Serenity
PRINCIPLES

STEPHEN D. HOWER

Serenity
PRINCIPLES

Biblical Direction That Will Change Your Life

SAINT LOUIS

Dedicated to my Lord and the partner He has given me in this ever changing life, my dear wife, Carol.

———◆◆◆———

Copyright © 1998 Concordia Publishing House
3558 S. Jefferson Avenue, St. Louis, MO 63118-3968
Manufactured in the United States of America

Library of Congress Cataloging-in-Publication Data

Hower, Stephen D., 1952-
    The serenity principles: biblical direction that will change your life / Stephen D. Hower.
      p. cm.
    ISBN 0-570-05335-8
     1. Peace of mind—Religious aspects—Christianity.
   2. Change—Religious aspects—Christianity. 3. Serenity prayer.
   I. Title
BV4908.5.H68 1998   98-17000
248.4—dc21

2 3 4 5 6 7 8 9 10   07 06 05 04 03 02 01 00 99 98

"Abide with Me"

Swift to its close ebbs out life's little day;
Earth's joys grow dim, its glories pass away;
Change and decay in all around I see;
O Thou who changest not, abide with me.

Henry Lyte (1793–1847)

Contents

Prologue

Q How many people does it take to change a lightbulb?
A At least three. One to change the bulb and at least two to discuss how good the old one was.

Q How many people does it take to change a lightbulb?
A None. We've grown accustomed to the dark.

Q How many people does it take to change a lightbulb?
A Change?

As the three answers imply, not everyone is pleased with the inevitability of change. Some people prefer the old days and old ways. Others resist change and settle for life under less than perfect conditions. They've gotten used to the dark. And still others, although unhappy with life, don't realize that change is possible.

The subject of change is a tough issue for almost everyone. Christians, unfortunately, aren't spared the heartache. We try to change, but we fail. Our human nature holds us back. Even the apostle Paul lamented, "I know that nothing good lives in me, that is, in my sinful nature. For I have the desire to do what is good, but I cannot carry it out. For what I do is not the good I want to do; no, the evil I do not want to do—this I keep on doing" (Romans 7:18–19).

How can change be accomplished when it is needed? Does God's Word offer any hope, direction, or power to make the changes you need to make?

Paul found the answer in Jesus. He wrote, "What a

wretched man I am! Who will rescue me from this body of death? Thanks be to God—through Jesus Christ our Lord!" (Romans 7:24–25). Jesus is *still* the answer. The Savior described Himself as "the way and the truth and the life" (John 14:6). This book is written for those who want to know how Jesus can change their lives for the better. The *Serenity Principles* are God's answers to your questions about change.

Introduction

God, grant me the serenity
to accept the things I cannot change,
Courage to change the things I can,
and wisdom to know the difference.

Unless You Change

This book is about change—desired change, inevitable change, and change to be opposed.

Change has happened on a routine basis with or without your consent your entire life. Those who've lived through the last century have seen dramatic changes in the way people live, work, and communicate:

- from horse-drawn carriages to horse-powered vehicles
- from oil lamps to baseball under the lights
- from sailing ships to supersonic jets
- from the telegraph to the Internet
- from a viewfinder to a satellite dish
- from flintlocks to smart bombs
- from root cellars to megastores
- from blacksmiths to robotics
- from binoculars to the Hubbell telescope
- from Pony Express to e-mail

These changes took years. How long will it take you to make a change?

Accomplishing desired change can be difficult—nearly impossible. Anyone who's ever tried to lose weight, break a bad habit, get out of debt, or achieve a difficult goal knows what Jesus meant when He said, "The spirit is willing, but the body is weak" (Matthew 26:41).

Other changes occur without any help at all. They can be unwanted, resisted, and strongly opposed, to no avail. They keep coming no matter how hard we resist them. Few people welcome the changes brought by aging, illness, job loss, an accident, or the death of a loved one. But denial is not the answer. Closing your eyes won't make the situation disappear.

Significant change requires intervention. Groups have been established around the world to give support, offer advice, and provide accountability to people trapped in habitual behavior. The Bible talks about such bondage to sin. Those who wrote the Bible experienced the same struggles we experience. Consider the desperate plight of the man who wrote these words:

> I know that nothing good lives in me, that is, in my sinful nature. For I have the desire to do what is good, but I cannot carry it out. For what I do is not the good I want to do; no, the evil I do not want to do—this I keep on doing. Now if I do what I do not want to do, it is no longer I who do it, but it is sin living in me that does it. So I find this law at work: When I want to do good, evil is right there with me. For in my inner being I delight in God's law; but I see another law at work in the members of my body, waging war against the law of my mind and making me a prisoner of the law of sin at work within my members. What a wretched man I am! Who will rescue me from this body of death?   (Romans 7:18–24)

Was the apostle really beyond his ability and in over his head? You bet. Did he live the rest of his life victimized by destructive behavior? No, he didn't.

What was the ultimate solution to his entrapment? How did he to make a change for the better? The next verse reveals the answer: "Thanks be to God—through Jesus Christ our Lord" (Romans 7:25). Therein lies our hope.

Have you tried everything else? Have you wondered how the Bible can help you overcome evil and obtain the victory? The *Serenity Principles* will help you discover God's promised relief. In His Word, you will find wisdom that leads from life abundant to life eternal.

Change for the Better Isn't 'Better' for Everyone

A life-changing improvement is often called a *breakthrough*— and by no mistake. Breakthrough is a positive word that calls attention to a significant discovery. Breakthroughs occur when someone looks at an old problem in a new way and discovers a new and better solution. The person literally breaks *through* the old paradigm to create a new and improved way of handling a difficult situation. Life gets better, easier, and more enjoyable because of breakthroughs. Despite the promise of better things, however, breakthroughs are often strongly resisted in favor of the status quo.

Why would anyone resist a better idea? It's quite simple: You can't experience a *breakthrough* without breaking something. Breakthroughs can be painful—broken hearts, broken homes, broken promises, broken dreams can lead to broken lives. Change-causing breakthroughs are hard on people, especially those with something to lose.

In January 1829, Martin Van Buren, governor of New York, wrote newly elected president Andrew Jackson an official letter of protest against progress.

January 31, 1829

President Jackson,

The canal system of this country is being threatened by the spread of a new form of transportation known as railroads. The federal government must preserve the canals for the following reasons.

One, if boats are supplanted by railroads, serious unemployment will result. Captains, cooks, drivers, hostlers, repairmen and lock tenders will be left without means of livelihood, not to mention the numerous farmers now employed in growing hay for horses.

Two, boat builders would suffer and towline, whip, and harness makers would be left destitute.

Three, canal boats are absolutely essential to the defense of the United States. In the event of the expected trouble with England, the Erie Canal would be the only means by which we could ever move the supplies so vital to waging modern war.

As you well know, Mr. President, railroad carriages are pulled at the enormous speeds of 15 miles per hour by engines which, in addition to endangering life and limb of passengers, roar and snort their way through the countryside, setting fire to crops, scaring the livestock and frightening women and children. The Almighty certainly never intended that people would travel at such breakneck speed.

Sincerely yours,

Martin Van Buren

Governor of New York[1]

Obviously Governor Van Buren and the Erie Canal that served his constituents were threatened by pending change. The Erie Canal was less than five years old and already in danger of becoming obsolete.

Change threatens those who have something to lose. From Governor Van Buren's perspective, his constituents' entire way of life was at stake. Personal loss is one of the main reasons people fear change.

Change can bring an end to a way of life, an end to friendship, an end to security, an end to status, an end to a beloved routine, an end to tradition. Change can endanger one's health and threaten even life itself. When things change, something of value often gets left behind. Take the telephone for instance—the basis of all modern communication. Not even its inventor was completely enamored of the change it brought. It wasn't long after his 1876 *breakthrough* that Alexander Graham Bell began to resent the invention's intrusion into his personal life. Preferring solitude to accessibility, Bell kept his own phone in a distant part of the house far from his personal study. When things change, something of personal value gets left behind.

Like It or Not, Change Is Inevitable

Change will come.

Only God "is the same yesterday and today and forever" (Hebrews 13:8). Therein lies the key. God, who made the heavens and the earth, has observed all the changes from the beginning. The One who doesn't change has seen it all. He gave Solomon the wisdom to understand, "What has been will be again; what has been done will be done again; there is nothing new under the sun. Is there anything of which one can say, 'Look! This is something new'? It was here already, long ago; it was here before our time" (Ecclesiastes 1:9–10). God knows all about change. So how does He help us? One way is through His Word.

The apostle Paul told young Timothy about the way: "You have known the holy Scriptures which are able to make you wise for salvation through faith in Christ Jesus. All Scripture is God-breathed and is useful for teaching, rebuking, correcting and training in righteousness, so that the man of God may be thoroughly equipped for every good work" (2 Timothy 3:15–17). We have places to go, people to see, and things to do along the road to heaven. The Lord wants us to accomplish them in the best possible way. In the inspired Scriptures, He has provided time-tested principles to help us accomplish all that He intends.

Understanding the *Serenity Principles* can make **change** a welcomed part of life.

Why Is It So Important to Understand Change?

Jesus said, "I tell you the truth, *unless you change* and become like little children, you will never enter the kingdom of heaven" (Matthew 18:3, emphasis added). Change is not merely a good idea, it is essential for eternal life. The Greek word Jesus chose to describe the change He requires is very specific. It means *to twist or turn around*. In other words, unless your life is *turned around*, and you acquire the simple faith of a child, you will never be counted among those who are saved. Obviously, left to ourselves we are headed in the wrong direction. Something very basic has to change in the heart of every man, woman, and child who wants to be saved. Such change is God's work and must be done God's way.

Getting the Help We Need

Change is God's business. He specializes in it. He changes people. He changes situations. He changes the weather. He changes the seasons. He causes the sun to rise in the east, run its course, and set in the west every day. (See Genesis 1:14–15.) The Bible says God alone makes the seasons to know their place. He alone maintains warehouses filled with ice, rain, and snow. He alone causes the thunder to rumble and the lightning to strike at His discretion. (See Job 36:32–33 and 38:22–30.) When it comes to change, wise people look to the Lord for direction.

Some Change Must Be Resisted at All Costs

In ancient Babylon a prideful king once commanded a destructive change throughout his kingdom. He erected a huge idol and required all his subjects to bow in reverence as a sign of submission. Those who refused to bow would be thrown into a fiery furnace. Three of God's servants knew this was a change they could not accept. Shadrach, Meshach, and Abednego told King Nebuchadnezzar, "the God we serve is able to save us …, and He will rescue us from your hand, O king. But even if He does not, we want you to know, O king, that we will not serve your gods or worship the image of gold you have set up" (Daniel 3:17–18). Those three young men had no idea what God *would* do, but they knew what God *could* do.

They trusted in the faithfulness of God, stood in the integrity of their faith, and were rescued from their enemy. They were prepared to die, but God had other plans. He used them to bring new life to a wayward king and his people.

Knowing God's will is essential when it comes to change.

God can help you accomplish necessary change, resist improper change, and cope with the inevitable changes of life. In the Bible you will find the wisdom of the One who has seen everything humankind has ever done. The *Serenity Principles* will help you develop a positive biblical perspective on change.

Even Change for the Better Can Be Hard

During my six years as the pastor of a congregation on the Gulf Coast of Texas, I often visited an elderly couple whose most active years were behind them. Charlie was so disabled by rheumatoid arthritis that he would rub his knees with horse liniment and wrap them with cloth diapers to neutralize the incessant pain. I was always careful to make Charlie the last of my homebound visits. He waited patiently all day for my arrival and would not let me leave until we'd shared a glass of sherry or a bottle of beer. After our devotional time, Emma served us food and filled our glasses while Charlie told me about the good old days. It was always a pleasure to visit Charlie and Emma.

Sometimes Charlie threw caution to the wind and escaped his prison. Charlie could not be easily dissuaded once his mind was set on escape. Despite his debilitating pain, he'd convince Emma to allow him to leave the shelter of their home for a half day's adventure. For the celebration of a friend's birthday or for certain Christian holidays, Charlie painfully walked whatever distance was required, leaning heavily on his walker, stopping for rest only when the pain became unbearable. Emma waited patiently by his side, coaxing but not hurrying her husband toward his goal. Until the very end, Charlie, although humble in every other respect, remained too proud to sit in a wheelchair except under extraordinary conditions. As the poet advised, Charlie was not about to go quietly into the night.

After Charlie's death, I watched Emma's life change dramatically. She began attending Bible classes and meetings that she had been unable to attend for the last several years. Before Charlie's health had become a factor, both of them had been active as leaders of various causes in their community and congregation. Emma quickly resumed her active role.

Once, in a quiet moment, I had the opportunity to ask Emma how she was coping with the change of being a widow. She smiled and remarked, "Oh, I miss Charlie terribly, even though I know we are both better off and it won't be long till I join him. You know, Pastor," she said with a twinkle in her eye, "there are days when I miss all the aggravation."

There are days when I miss all the aggravation. Emma's honest assessment explains just how ingrained even undesirable activity can become. Not every change for the better is easily accepted.

So what do you do? Change happens—how will you handle it? Can God help you make needed change? What power does God offer that will enable you to cope with inevitable change? How can you maintain Christian values and beliefs in a changing world of compromise? *Serenity Principles* will help you "so that when the day of evil comes, you may be able to stand your ground, and after you have done everything, to stand" (Ephesians 6:13).

The Changeless Christ

Henry F. Lyte was born in Ednam, Ireland, just a few years after America won its independence from England. A bright young man, Lyte intended to enter the medical profession, but God had different plans. Lyte studied for the ministry and at the early age of 22 was ordained an Anglican clergyman. Two hundred years later Lyte's work is still remembered because of a dramatic personal change brought about through the death of a close friend and fellow clergyman.

As his friend lay critically ill, Lyte searched the Scriptures to understand God's purpose and to comfort his friend. He wrote, "I was greatly affected by the whole matter and brought to look at life and its issue with a different eye than before; and I began to study my Bible and preach in another manner than I had previously done."[2]

God doesn't always change situations, but He can use any situation to change people. Lyte's renewed commitment didn't result in sudden wealth and prosperity. He lived in poverty his entire life, but he kept his vow to provide for his friend's children. The pastor's life was difficult, but out of the refiner's fire came pure gold. Who hasn't been moved by the words of his famous poem, "Abide with Me"? The second stanza reveals his secret to handling inevitable change through faith in the One who never changes.

> Swift to its close ebbs out life's little day;
> Earth's joys grow dim, its glories pass away.
> Change and decay in all around I see;
> O Thou who changest not, abide with me.[3]

Lyte's health was never strong. The dampness of his coastal parish undermined his frailty. He traveled to the continent in hope of recovery but died in Nice, France, on November 20, 1847. How did he handle life's ultimate transition? Did the Lord hold His cross before his closing eyes? Did Lyte's Savior shine through the gloom and point him to the skies?[4] Those present said Lyte's final words were, "Peace; joy!"[5] The changeless Christ helped His servant accomplish the necessary change.

New Life in Christ Is Not an Empty Promise

Jesus told a wise and highly respected teacher of His day, "I tell you the truth, no one can see the kingdom of God unless he is born again" (John 3:3). Although the words *born again* have become quite popular, the Greek words Jesus used to describe what must happen are more specific than that. Literally translated, the Greek words *annothen gennao* mean "born from above." Jesus told Nicodemus that he couldn't understand God's ways unless he was *born from above*. Nicodemus asked how this could be possible: "How can a man be born when he is old?" (John 3:4). Jesus was talking about a miracle that only God can do. He told Nicodemus it's like the wind: "[It] blows wherever it pleases. You hear its sound, but you cannot tell where it comes from or where it is going. So it is with everyone born of the Spirit" (John 3:8).

Jesus was telling Nicodemus that change is God's business. Nicodemus would have to accept by faith that which he could not see and could not completely understand. It is like the wind. And like the wind, you will notice the effect.

This book is about change—the change God can and does accomplish in the lives of His children. The *Serenity Principles* are taken from God's Word to bring God's power to bear in the lives of God's children. Change, after all, is God's business.

Part 1

Coming to Grips
with Change

Things We Can Change

I'm gonna make a change for once in my life
It's gonna feel real good
It's gonna make a difference ... gonna make it right.

I'm talking to the man in the mirror.
I'm asking him to make a change.
No message could have been any clearer,
"If you wanna make the world a better place,
take a look at yourself,
and make a *change!*"[6]

Michael Jackson sang those words in a powerful song about the importance of personal change. Jackson was right. Every important change begins with a decision. To be more accurate, meaningful change is rarely accomplished by *one* good decision—it takes many.

So why don't we change? Why is it so hard to give up chocolate, quit cigarettes, avoid snacks, say no to salt, keep our exercise schedules, conduct home devotions, and call home to Mom?

Can a man trapped by pornography ever be free? Is alcohol addiction really forever? Can runaway spending be curbed? Can workaholics achieve balance? Can the agoraphobic woman recover to live a normal life? Why doesn't our "talk with the man in the mirror" achieve the desired outcome? Why can't we just *make a change*? Is it impossible?

The Impossible Is Possible

The Colorado River flows 1,400 miles from its headwaters, 14,000 feet high in the Rocky Mountains, to its final destination in the Gulf of California. For many years the river had a violent reputation. Its rapids and waterfalls were so dangerous it remained largely unexplored and inaccessible long after the surrounding country was mapped and charted. Spanish explorers named it Rio Colorado (River of Red) because its turbulent waters were rarely clear of silt and minerals carried along in its powerful grasp. How strong could the river be? Every 24 hours it carried an average of one million tons of sand, silt, gravel, and rock past any given point. Who could possibly tame the wild Colorado?

That's exactly how many people feel about making a change. Victimized by the powerful grip of a greater force, they remain helpless and hopeless in the grasp of their invisible enemy. Unable to reach the safety of the distant shore, the victims of unchanging circumstance remain trapped in the currents of status quo. Without rescue many will drown in despair. For them, serenity is illusive. The green pastures and still waters promised by the psalmist (Psalm 23:2) remain just out of reach.

The Danger of Isolation

So there you are—isolated, trapped in the currents, about to drown. Those who need help are often the last to seek it. The very thing that enslaves also isolates. Their inability to change sweeps them battered and beaten along life's rock-strewn rapids.

The Colorado River is as isolated as a river can get. Its waters are buried deep between canyon walls so formidable there is virtually no natural access to the riverbed for 90 percent of its journey. The Grand Canyon's walls shield the river's life-giving sustenance from the thirsty deserts through which it flows. Some of the canyon's sheer cliffs rise more than 5,000 feet straight up. Isolated, foaming, churning, twisting, and gouging its way toward the sea, the river's potential seemed forever unattainable.

But there are those who believe virtually impossible things are, by definition, possible. Some of those visionaries vowed to tame the destructive forces of the untamable river. It would not be easy. The Colorado River system drains a quarter million square miles of land in seven states. It was difficult to reach, impossible to navigate, and a long way from everywhere, flowing through one of North America's least populated regions. Taming the Colorado would require herculean effort and a determination unmatched by any engineering feat of its day.

And what was virtually impossible has been accomplished. On September 30, 1935, President Franklin D. Roosevelt officially dedicated a dam so massive its size and design still amaze those who cross the state line between Arizona and Nevada over its 726-foot-high span. More important, the impressive dam brought an end to the Colorado's unrealized potential. The river now provides precious drinking water to a growing population, generates 4 billion kilowatt-hours of electricity annually, and irrigates more than 1.5 million acres of land in the United States and Mexico. Where only sagebrush and cactus once grew, farmers now harvest vegetables, fruit, wheat, hay, and cotton.

When I first saw Hoover Dam I marveled not only at its size, but also at the vision and logistics required for such an enormous undertaking. Four and a quarter million cubic yards of concrete holding back 35 million cubic meters of water (9.2 trillion gallons, or nearly two years of the river's average annual flow) reaching 110 miles upstream at depths up to 500 feet!

Significant change is possible but not easy. There is nothing easy about accomplishing a virtually impossible goal, whether taming a raging river or overcoming a personal limitation. The taming of the Colorado River required significant sacrifice: 94 construction workers and two government employees were killed between 1931 and 1937 while working on the dam. The sacrifices you make for the changes in your life most likely won't be as great, but they'll be sacrifices just the same. And God will enable you to make the change: "Because He Himself suffered when He was tempted, He is able to help those who are being tempted" (Hebrews 2:18).

Need Drives Change

Two overwhelming needs inspired the taming of the Colorado River and the construction of Hoover Dam. First, its raging waters were unpredictable and destroyed both people and property. Second, its waters were an important resource that held hope for millions who needed the electricity the river could generate.

In a similar way the pain and potential of life motivate people to make significant change. Ending the pain and accomplishing God's intended purpose are strong reasons to change.

Personal resolve to accomplish needed change or to adjust to a difficult situation will not automatically accomplish the results Christians desire. Desiring is not enough. Simply vowing to change a situation, attitude, behavior, or lifestyle is no guarantee of success. So where do we begin?

Potential Benefits Are Strong Motivation

The Bible offers the example of Christ and His sacrifice as an encouragement for dealing with the difficulty of change. It tells us to "throw off everything that hinders and the sin that so easily entangles, and let us run with perseverance the race marked out for us" (Hebrews 12:1). But how? After dedicating an entire chapter to a description of the sacrifices made by the heroes of the Old Testament, the apostle continued his letter to the Hebrews by urging, "Let us fix our eyes on Jesus, the author and perfecter of our faith, who for the joy set before Him endured the cross, scorning its shame, and sat down at the right hand of the throne of God" (Hebrews 12:2). Jesus accomplished His difficult task because of *the joy set before* Him. The benefits and potential joy of a new life in Christ are great incentives to motivate change.

Jesus once asked a rich young man to make a change in his life. The story is told in Matthew 19:16–30. The man was morally upright, a respected citizen. He believed in God and accepted God's standards summarized by the Ten Commandments. On one particular day he came to Jesus with a question. "Teacher," he said, "what good thing must I do to get eternal life?" (Matthew 19:16).

He had asked an important question. It was the kind of question that caused nearby disciples to gather close and listen with greater interest. Despite his impeccable moral record, the young man lacked the serenity that comes from being right with God. He desired the kind of peace everyone wants but few possess. "How do I get right with God? What can I do to make myself acceptable?" Maybe deep inside he knew that avoidance of sin was not enough. He sensed something still lacking. Something needed to be done. But maybe not. Perhaps he felt quite good about himself and wanted confirmation from a holy man. Whatever the reason, he put his question to Jesus. Since the death of John the Baptist, Jesus had developed a reputation as a miracle worker and teacher of truth unlike any other. (See John 3:2 and Matthew 7:28–29.) If He would assure the young man of his goodness, maybe those nagging doubts would vanish.

As He often did, Jesus answered the young man's question with a question of His own. "Why do you ask Me about what is good? There is only one who is good" (Matthew 19:17). The young man's question was to the point, but Jesus' question was more so. It was a question He had recently asked His own disciples, "Who do people say that the Son of Man is? … Who do you say that I am?" (Matthew 16:13–15). (Note: Before you ask questions about eternal life, you better know who you're talking to!) Jesus reminded the young man that only One was qualified to answer his question. Only God could spell out the requirements for life. Then, as if to show that He was God and qualified to explain the expectations of heaven, Jesus continued. "If you want to enter eternal life, obey the commandments" (Matthew 19:17).

This is where the encounter gets interesting. "Which ones?" the man inquired. Jesus replied, " 'Do not murder, do not commit adultery, do not steal, do not give false testimony, honor your father 'and' mother, and love your neighbor as yourself' " (Matthew 19:18–19). It was the opportunity the young man had waited for. In front of God and everyone he was able to say with all sincerity, "All these I have kept." But then, as if still uncertain, he asked, "What do I still lack?" (Matthew 19:20).

What do I still lack? We should admire his honesty. He was troubled by an indescribable sense of inadequacy. Something was lacking, but he couldn't put his finger on it. His best efforts didn't seem to be enough. "I've lived a good life. I've avoided the rabble and their parties. My life is above reproach. I'm fair in my dealings. I would never intentionally hurt any-body. I'm not the kind to lie, cheat, or steal. My parents are proud of me. My friends can count on me. What do I still lack?" The young man was good at asking questions. His honesty with Jesus received an honest reply. "If you want to be perfect, go, sell your possessions and give to the poor, and you will have treasure in heaven. Then come, follow Me" (Matthew 19:21).

Not fair! The young man was willing to do anything with-in reason, but Jesus had asked too much. Did the young man hear Jesus correctly? Change is one thing, perfection is some-thing else. Did Jesus really say *if you want to be perfect*? Who can be perfect? Even if the young man agreed, even if he sold everything and gave all he owned to the poor, he could never be perfect.

Matthew was standing nearby with the rest of the disci-ples. He was so astonished he wrote down what happened next. "When the young man heard this, he went away sad, because he had great wealth" (Matthew 19:22). End of discus-sion, end of story—point, game, match. Not yet. The most important part of the story occurred after the rich man turned and walked away.

Like the man before them, the disciples couldn't believe their ears. How could Jesus require anyone to be perfect? No one was perfect. Didn't King David commit adultery and then murder Uriah to cover up his sin? Didn't Moses disobey God in the wilderness and Elijah suffer from doubt? Now it was the disciples who had a question. "They were greatly aston-ished and asked, 'Who then can be saved?' " (Matthew 19:25).

Does the change you're facing seem impossible? Those

struggling with impossible situations need to listen carefully to Jesus' answer. "With man this is impossible, but with God all things are possible" (Matthew 19:26).

Jesus admits it. The change He asks of all who want eternal life is impossible. We can't do it. Like the young man, our best is never good enough. What Jesus asks, God must provide. Jesus was asking for the impossible! He still does.

Herein lies the key to change: What God asks of you, God enables you to accomplish.

You Are Not Alone

Ignacy Jan Paderewski is acclaimed as one of the world's greatest composers and pianists. Although born in the obscurity of Russian Poland in 1860, he rose to world fame. By age 12 he was performing public recitals. By age 19 he was appointed full professor at the Warsaw Conservatory. His music and concerts were heard in Paris, London, and the great cities of America, where he lived in retirement until his death in 1941.

The story is told of an English working woman who once took her 8-year-old son to hear the great master play a recital at the Concert Hall of London. She hoped that by hearing Paderewski her son would be inspired to a renewed interest and greater dedication to his study of music. It was an important evening in a great city. The concert hall was electric in anticipation of the maestro's entrance.

The impressive stage was empty except for the presence of the highly polished and impeccably tuned concert piano. There would be no distractions. Everyone had come for only one purpose: to hear the master play. The young boy's mother, eager with anticipation, entered a conversation with someone near her. Without his mother's knowledge, the young boy slipped quietly down the aisle, his eyes fixed on the stage. The piano beckoned the young student until his hands rested on the ivory keys. In shaky, childish fashion he began plunking out the familiar sound of "Chopsticks."

The audience gasped in social horror. How could such a thing happen? Who would bring such an unruly child to such a sophisticated evening as this? Where was the child's mother? Something had to be done and quickly. It was.

As the child's mother rushed forward with as much dignity as anyone under such duress could muster, another figure emerged from the wings of the stage. Soon the garish clatter of "Chopsticks" was overlaid with the beautiful sounds of a contrasting melody. Upon hearing the clatter from just offstage, the quick-thinking Paderewski slipped through the curtains and joined the brave young musician at the keyboard. Surprised and expecting the worst, the boy's hands faltered, but Paderewski urged him on. Together the master and the novice orchestrated a thing of beauty.[7]

The presence of the master's hands made all the difference.

Likewise, we are not alone in our struggle with human frailty. What is impossible for us alone is possible for us in Christ. Both virgin Mary's and Elizabeth's pregnancies were beyond the possibility of mere humans. The angel Gabriel offered the only explanation. He told Mary, "Nothing is impossible with God" (Luke 1:37).

Total Reliance and Daily Provision

The apostle Paul learned the same lesson half a century later. His weakness haunted him. He pleaded with God to intervene and grant permanent and complete relief. If God would remove his weakness and grant the needed strength, Paul reasoned it would be enough.

God's answer then is the same today. "My grace is sufficient for you, for My power is made perfect in weakness" (2 Corinthians 12:9). The task was accomplished by God working through Paul's weakness, not by Paul directing God's power.

Daily dependence and total reliance on God are lessons the Lord requires all His children to learn. For good reason both principles have become pillars in every 12-step recovery program for compulsive behavior. God will not make us independent when dependence on Him is our greatest need. Paul wrote, "I have learned the secret of being content in any and every situation, whether well fed or hungry, whether living in plenty or in want. I can do everything through Him who gives me strength" (Philippians 4:12–13).

In life there are many virtually impossible situations that need changing. If your life falls into that category, the Bible has good news. What God asks of us, He also enables us to do. His "Bureau of Reclamation" makes the U.S. Department of the Interior's taming of the Colorado look like child's play. If your life is in need of reclamation and redirection, you've come to the right place. The serenity principles of Scripture are the key to "the peace of God, which transcends all understanding" (Philippians 4:7).

So what do you want to change? Do you want to stop smoking? stick with an exercise program? get out of an abusive situation? Do you feel isolated? Do you feel that the task is impossible? It's not—if you ask for God's help and guidance. Work through this next section to understand how God can work through your struggles and help you identify what you can do to change your life for the better.

Taking Time for Reflection and Personal Growth

Be still, and know that I am God. Psalm 46:10

1. Read of Paul's frustrations in Romans 7:15–25.
   - Have you ever felt like Paul?
   - What does Paul describe as his only hope?
2. Read Psalm 13.
   - Describe David's frame of mind.
   - What is the difference between the way Paul felt and the way David felt?
   - How does the psalmist conclude his thoughts?
3. Identify an aspect of your life that needs change.
   - How will you practice daily reliance on God in this area of your life to accomplish change?

Pray about Things You Can Change

Gracious Lord, Your Word says, "Every good and perfect gift is from above, coming down from the Father of the heavenly lights, who *does not change* like shifting shadows" (James 1:17, emphasis added). Lord, I live in the land of shifting shadows. I have my share of struggles. I'm not the person I want to be, and I'm certainly not living up to Your expectations. I'm not asking You to remove my struggle, but keep me from the Evil One. Through my weakness, demonstrate Your strength. Help me trust You for all that I need today. Forgive, renew, and restore me by Your grace. Be my anchor, Lord, and hear my prayer for the sake of Jesus, my Savior. Amen.

Things We Can't Change

S ome things never change!" Those were the words Mom typically used to express her disappointment over some new trouble I had instigated at school. She was never surprised by the news that I was in trouble, but she was always hopeful that someday I'd change.

I attended a small Christian grade school. If I remember correctly, there were only nine people in my graduating class. During most of those years, the school had only three classrooms. The first two grades were taught by Mrs. Bippus; grades 3, 4, and 5 were taught by Mr. Trzynka; and the rest were assigned to Mr. Janetzke, who also served as principal. There were fewer than 100 children in the entire school, so the seven Howers made up about 10 percent of the school's population. It was not unusual to have two or three Howers in one room. From my perspective, that was *not* a good thing.

In such a close-knit environment, it was impossible for a person to keep many secrets from his parents. If I failed to complete an assignment, didn't know my memory work, or got a whoopin' from Mr. Trzynka, my brothers and sisters would literally sprint off the bus for the privilege of being the first to tell Mom. (I always took my time getting off the bus.)

Unfortunately, my older brothers and sisters were obedient and respectful students, the kind teachers praise at parent-teacher conferences. I wasn't exactly incorrigible, but no one was ever surprised to hear I'd spent time in the cloak-hall awaiting Mr. Trzynka and his razor strap.

But taking "licks" from Mr. Trzynka was the least of my worries. Spending the rest of the day knowing I'd be ratted on by my own flesh and blood put a real damper on things. A spanking at school almost always meant some form of punishment at home.

In those days, parents held teachers in pretty high regard. If a teacher gave their child a spanking, my parents assumed it was for a good reason. My twisted explanations never carried much weight with Mom or Dad. Depending on the infraction (and how well my brother or sister exaggerated the matter) I was banned from television, which meant I would miss an important episode of *The Mickey Mouse Club* or *The Adventures of Superman*. If the infraction involved disrespectful behavior, I'd almost certainly receive another spanking and be made to sit in a chair for an hour or so. If sitting in a chair meant I could watch television, I preferred a spanking over being sent to my room.

My youngest son, Jacob, is surely an answer to my mother's unspoken prayer. Now, when I hear my wife, Carol, respond to Jacob's latest exploit with the words, "Some things never change," I smile quietly to myself. I have to be careful. If Carol ever caught me openly smiling, I'd be sent to my room or be grounded with Jacob for the rest of my life. Some things never change.

The well-known Serenity Prayer begins by asking God to help us with unchanging things. We pray, "God, grant me the serenity to accept the things I cannot change ..." Much about life falls into the category of things we can't change. This chapter groups unchangeable things into four categories: human nature, the past, other people, and God, who the Bible describes as "the same yesterday and today and forever" (Hebrews 13:8).

Human Nature Does Not Change

Like many Christians, I enjoy listening to Christian radio. Sometimes, I must admit, I don't know whether to smile or cry over the pessimistic assessment of the future that pre-occupies so many religious programs. Too many Christians experience great discouragement from the constant clarion call of well-meaning Christian leaders attempting to "return America to its Christian heritage." While I applaud their evan-gelical zeal and agree Christians are to be the salt and light of their communities, the Bible predicts society will get worse, not better, before the coming of the Lord:

> Jesus said, "At that time many will turn away from the faith
> and will betray and hate each other, and many false
> prophets will appear and deceive many people. Because of
> the increase of wickedness, the love of most will grow cold,
> but he who stands firm to the end will be saved."
>
> (Matthew 24:10–13)

It should not surprise us that conditions on earth (even in America) are on a downward spiral toward destruction. While it is sad and disconcerting to watch human nature run its course, it should not surprise or overly depress us. Jesus went on to say, "When these things begin to take place, stand up and lift up your heads, because your redemption is drawing near" (Luke 21:28).

Bad news for some is good news for others. The Bible even says the saints in heaven are looking forward to the day of their vindication (see Revelation 6:10). The concluding prayer of all Scripture pleads, "Amen. Come, Lord Jesus" (Revelation 22:20).

Until the Lord comes, Christians are going to have to

accept the truth about human nature and the world in which we live:

- This is not the world God intended. (See Romans 8:19ff.)
- Most people are not Christian. (See Matthew 7:13–14.)
- Even Christians fall short of God's standards. (See Romans 3:22–23.)
- Our own sinful human nature will continue to frustrate us in this life. (See Romans 7:18–20.)

These things aren't going to change.

God is well aware of our human limitations. We're reminded of that in the Psalms, especially in Psalm 103, which is one of my favorites. I was honored to read it at my father's memorial service. It tells us to maintain an "attitude of gratitude" throughout life. It also reminds us that God understands the limitation of human nature and treats us with compassion:

> The LORD is compassionate and gracious, slow to anger, abounding in love. He will not always accuse, nor will He harbor His anger forever; He does not treat us as our sins deserve or repay us according to our iniquities. For as high as the heavens are above the earth, so great is His love for those who fear Him; as far as the east is from the west, so far has He removed our transgressions from us. As a father has compassion on His children, so the LORD has compassion on those who fear Him; for He knows how we are formed, He remembers that we are dust.
> (Psalm 103:8–14)

He does not treat us as our sins deserve or repay us according to our iniquities. ... He remembers that we are dust. God knows the limitations of our human nature and because of His compassion and mercy, He will not always accuse, nor will He harbor His anger forever. God's love is so great He doesn't limit it to Christians. He allows His blessing to be experienced and shared even by nonbelievers. Jesus said, "He causes His sun to rise on the evil and the good, and sends rain on the righteous and the unrighteous" (Matthew 5:45). He is truly a compassionate God.

After the earth was destroyed by a flood in the days of Noah, God put a rainbow in the heavens as a reminder to everyone that He would restrain His anger despite the sinfulness of His people. The reason He gave for His decision is similar to the words of Psalm 103. He said, "Never again will I curse the ground because of man, even though every inclination of his heart is evil from childhood. And never again will I destroy all living creatures, as I have done. 'As long as the earth endures, seedtime and harvest, cold and heat, summer and winter, day and night will never cease' " (Genesis 8:21–22). Don't fail to notice the qualifying phrase, *as long as the earth endures*. His mercy and patience will not last forever. The Bible reminds us,

> *The whole world [will be] held accountable to God.*
> *Therefore no one will be declared righteous in His sight*
> *by observing the law; rather, through the law we become*
> *conscious of sin. But now a righteousness [perfection] from*
> *God, apart from law, has been made known, to which the*
> *Law and the Prophets testify. This righteousness from God*
> *comes through faith in Jesus Christ to all who believe.*
> (Romans 3:19–22)

Wow! God not only understands our weak human nature and tolerates our sinfulness, He did something about it. Because we could not save ourselves by keeping His commandments perfectly, He sent a Savior who could. Jesus accomplished what our sinful nature could never achieve. He kept the Law perfectly and then suffered God's judgment as our substitute. No other person could have accomplished this for us. (See Psalm 49:7–8.) Because He was Immanuel—God with us—He could die for the sins of all people.

The Bible makes an important point about our new status as redeemed children of God. Paul concluded, "What, then, shall we say in response to this? If God is for us, who can be against us? He who did not spare His own Son, but gave Him up for us all—how will He not also, along with Him, graciously give us all things?" (Romans 8:31–32). In other words, if God loved us and sent Jesus to die for us while we were lost in sin, just imagine what He will do now that we have been purified through forgiveness!

While our sinful human nature limits our ability to be all that we want to be, and can cause us to do things we regret, it should never drive us to despair and depression. While we must deal with our sinful nature until we enter heaven, it helps to remember these three important lessons about human nature:

1. God understands our human limitations and accepts sinners as we are.
2. Jesus died to overcome our sinfulness and make those who believe in Him perfect in the sight of His Father.
3. If God loved us before our redemption, how much more will He care for us now that Christ has redeemed us from all sin?

We Can't Change the Past

Everyone has a past. Before I entered the seminary and was ordained as a Christian pastor I worked all kinds of jobs. I carried newspapers, worked as a clerk in a dairy store, and, during the winter, shoveled salt into a spreader box attached to the back of a flatbed truck. I worked in manholes in public sewers running connecting rods through drainpipes. One summer I emptied garbage cans into the back of a city garbage truck. During seminary years I signed on as a mover's helper and loaded furniture into semitrailers. I ran a printing press, worked in kitchens washing pots and pans, and pushed a mop or two as a college custodian. Whatever job fit my schedule and could help pay the tuition, I was ready, willing, and able to take.

One of my all-time favorite jobs was working for the Erie Lackawanna Railroad. The division headquarters for the railroad was in my hometown. My grandpa Hower had been an engineer in the old days of steam locomotives, and my childhood home was only a short walk from the railyard. Members of my home church, including my brother-in-law, worked on the railroad and helped me get summer work there during my junior and senior years of college. The first year I was a "gandydancer," working on a section gang assigned to repair and improve the tracks. The second summer I rode the trains as a brakeman.

Our section crew used special tools to carry the 39-foot-long steel rails, huge wrenches to tighten bolts, pry-bars and special sledge hammers designed to drive spikes into pressure-treated ties. One of the instruments we used was a gauge to determine the exact spacing between rails. The U.S. standard railroad gauge is exactly 4 feet, 8½ inches wide. It always struck me as an odd measurement. Why not 5 feet or even 4½ feet? Why 4 feet, 8½ inches wide?

On the surface the answer to the strange measurement is fairly straightforward. The American rail system is 4 feet, 8½ inches wide because that was the gauge used in England. But why is such an odd measurement used in England? It is certainly not based on any standard metric distance. The English gauge was based on the same measurements they used to build horse-drawn wagons. So why were wagon wheels separated by such an odd measurement? The explanation may surprise you.

> *If they tried to use any other spacing the wagons would break on some of the old, long distance roads, because that's the spacing of the old wheel ruts. So who built these old rutted roads? The first long distance roads in Europe were built by Imperial Rome for the benefit of their legions. The roads have been used ever since. And the ruts? The initial ruts, which everyone else had to match for fear of destroying their wagons were made by Roman war chariots. Since the chariots were made for or by Imperial Rome they were all alike in the matter of wheel spacing. ... The Imperial Roman chariots were made just wide enough to accommodate the back-ends of two war horses.*[10]

The past has a way of hanging around. We can change our present, we can change our future, but there is nothing we can change about our past. The past lives on in many ways, some of them wonderful, some not so wonderful.

It is no different for Christians. Many of us were raised by nonbelievers. We had alcoholic fathers, watched our parents divorce, lost loved ones in car accidents, suffered child abuse, or lost jobs through no fault of our own. Some of us made horrible mistakes and are still living with the consequences. We aren't alone. Some of the great heroes of the faith had a past:

- To save his own skin Abraham lied about Sarah being his wife.
- Jacob cheated his brother out of his inheritance.
- Job lost his entire family in a natural disaster.

- Moses once put more faith in a stick than in the promise of God.
- Saul lied to a prophet.
- David committed adultery and murdered to cover it up.
- Solomon worshiped false gods with his unbelieving wives.
- Peter lied about being a friend of Jesus.

But God doesn't focus on the past. When He forgives, He forgets. Why do we beat ourselves up with wrongs and mistakes that God has long ago forgotten? The devil—not God—loves to remind Christians of their past failures and troubles. The Lord has perfect amnesia when it comes to mistakes. Here's how the Bible describes God's treatment of forgiven sin:

- "As far as the east is from the west, so far has He removed our transgressions from us." (Psalm 103:12, emphasis added)
- "In Your love You kept me from the pit of destruction; You have put all my sins behind Your back." (Isaiah 38:17, emphasis added)
- "I, even I, am He who blots out your transgressions, for My own sake, and remembers your sins no more." (Isaiah 43:25, emphasis added)
- "I will forgive their wickedness and will remember their sins no more." (Jeremiah 31:34, emphasis added)
- "In those days, at that time," declares the LORD, "search will be made for Israel's guilt, but there will be none, and for the sins of Judah, but none will be found, for I will forgive the remnant I spare." (Jeremiah 50:20, emphasis added)
- "You will tread our sins underfoot and hurl all our iniquities into the depths of the sea." (Micah 7:19, emphasis added)

Maybe one of the reasons we don't understand the way God forgives sin is because we don't think like He does. When people wrong us we may forgive them, but we're not likely to forget it. It makes me shudder when I pray, "Father, forgive my sins in the same way I forgive others." I really don't want the Lord to forgive my sins like I forgive others who sin against me. I prefer better treatment. The way God forgives us should have an impact on the way we treat others and ourselves. We can't change the past, but neither should we dwell on it—God doesn't.

Moving On to the Future

Paul learned the lesson of grace in a very personal way. He had been used by Satan to arrest, jail, and execute many early Christians. Paul was not one to do a job halfheartedly. He poured himself into his work. It must have been painful for him to recall his past. He wrote to the Christians in Galatia, "You have heard of my previous way of life in Judaism, how intensely I persecuted the church of God and tried to destroy it. I was advancing in Judaism beyond many Jews of my own age and was extremely zealous for the traditions of my fathers" (Galatians 1:13–14). He called himself the *chief of sinners* (See 1 Timothy 1:15 KJV).

The difference between Paul and most Christians is that Paul used his past to make a difference in his future. He didn't hide his past from anyone. He told the young pastor Timothy, "I was shown mercy so that in me, the worst of sinners, Christ Jesus might display His unlimited patience as an example for those who would believe on Him and receive eternal life" (1 Timothy 1:16).

We are not fully released from our past until we can talk openly about it. When mistakes and abuses of our past can be used to tell of the grace and mercy of God, then our past has no power over us. As long as Satan can use our past to create guilt, shame, anger, and bitterness we will lack the serenity God wants us to experience. Paul knew how Satan could trouble people with their past. He once told his secret to success:

> I *press on to take hold of that for which Christ Jesus took hold of me. Brothers, I do not consider myself yet to have taken hold of it. But one thing I do*: Forgetting what is behind and straining toward what is ahead, I *press on toward the goal to win the prize for which God has called me heavenward in Christ Jesus.*
> (*Philippians* 3:12–14, *emphasis added*)

The future—not the past—was the focus of Paul's attention. He makes a good point. Why beat yourself up over something you can't change and which God has forgotten?

Changing Other People

S tandard operating procedure in premarital counseling is to identify those things about a potential spouse that one or both counselees are trying to change. Although the question usually takes a more subtle form, what the counselor wants to know is, "If you could change one thing about your future spouse, what would it be?" The answers may range from tidiness to punctuality. Sometimes they can be more serious, such as hoping the potential spouse will become more faithful or see the need for responsible work habits. Usually the counselor will try to help the couple understand the danger of marrying someone with the intention of changing him or her.

We can't change others. We can, however, change ourselves. By changing our behavior we exert a great deal of influence on those closest to us. In the great relational chapter of 1 Peter, the apostle offered advice to Christian wives: "Wives, in the same way be submissive to your husbands so that, if any of them do not believe the word, they may be won over without words by the behavior of their wives, when they see the purity and reverence of your lives" (1 Peter 3:1–2).

Peter's advice is no guarantee that husbands will admire their wives' behavior and accept God's will in their lives. People after all are free agents. (Not even the kindest treatment of the Lord could keep Adam and Eve from exercising their free will against His clear warning.) Peter has struck upon a principle, however, that every Christian should understand. It is the same advice Paul offered in his letter to the Romans:

> Do not repay anyone evil for evil. Be careful to do what
> is right in the eyes of everybody. If it is possible, as far
> as it depends on you, live at peace with everyone. Do not
> take revenge, my friends, but leave room for God's wrath,
> for it is written: "It is mine to avenge; I will repay,"
> says the Lord. On the contrary: "If your enemy is hungry,
> feed him; if he is thirsty, give him something to drink.
> In doing this, you will heap burning coals on his head."
> Do not be overcome by evil, but overcome evil with good.
> (Romans 12:17–21)

Paul offers us advice on dealing with others that explains what we can do, what we can't do, and how God will help.

1. Control yourself. Don't take revenge.

2. Let there be nothing in your behavior that justifies their continued misbehavior.

3. Realize the outcome isn't completely under your control. Paul said, *as far as it depends on you.*

4. Turn it over to the Lord and expect Him to get involved.

5. Overcome evil with good.

The advice is pretty clear. Look again at the fourth point. It is no small thing to turn someone's behavior over to the Lord. Taking personal injustice to the courts of the Lord is not the same as doing nothing.

When Saul tried to kill David out of jealousy, David refused to take matters into his own hands. He told Saul, "May the LORD judge between you and me. And may the LORD avenge the wrongs you have done to me, but my hand will not touch you" (1 Samuel 24:12). We know how that turned out. The Lord removed Saul from his throne and established an everlasting covenant with the household of David.

When it comes to the behavior of others, know what you can do and what you can't do. You *can* change yourself. You take the injustice to God in prayer. It is even possible that your kind response could ultimately affect the outcome for the better. But finally each person will be accountable before the Lord for his or her own behavior.

God Doesn't Change

L ast, but not least, we must affirm *God does not change*. This is one of the major differences between God and man. The prophet Samuel once told Saul, "He who is the Glory of Israel does not lie or change His mind; for He is not a man, that He should change His mind" (1 Samuel 15:29). Saul changed his mind often and expected God to do the same. He was sadly mistaken. When God spoke, it was with certainty.

Consistency is important. As we study the serenity principles, knowing that God is "the same yesterday and today and forever" (Hebrews 13:8) gives credibility to His counsel. He didn't work through certain principles in the Old Testament, different principles in the New Testament, and leave us guessing about how He will respond today or tomorrow. He is the Rock that cannot be moved. When God takes a stand, offers advice, or makes a promise, Christians can act with certainty. The Scripture confirms it, "[God] does not change like shifting shadows" (James 1:17).

Some things are beyond our control: our past, human nature, and the behavior of others. But not even these things are outside God's control. As the Serenity Prayer reminds us, the key to our peace of mind is knowing the difference.

Taking Time for Reflection and Personal Growth

Be still, and know that I am God. Psalm 46:10

1. Read Psalm 103:7–13.
   - What do these verses say about our sinful nature?
   - What do they say about God in relation to our sinful nature?
2. Although we can't change others, what change can we make that may bring about change in others?
   - Read the description of attitudes that come by virtue of God's Spirit in Galatians 5:22–25. How might these attitudes bring about change in relationships you have with other people?
3. What are some things in your life that you can't change?
   - How does that affect your daily living?
   - Stop and pray. Turn these things over to God and expect Him to get involved.

Pray about Things You Can't Change

Father, the hymn writer called You *Thou who changest not*. I'm glad You don't change, Lord. I can count on You to love me the same yesterday, today, and tomorrow. There are things about me that I wish I could change, Lord. I sin every day, and I will continue to do so until I die. By the indwelling of Your Holy Spirit, help me to overcome my sinful nature and become spiritually mature and Christlike in my daily activities. Likewise, help me to be more accepting of the sinful nature of others around me. Help me to look beyond their behavior and love them as You love me—unconditionally. Through Jesus Christ, my Savior. Amen.

Change We Can't Avoid

The experts tell us, "When the paradigm shifts, everyone goes back to zero." In other words, when life takes a sharp turn off the well-traveled path of our experience, all the lessons we've learned and the all the knowledge we've acquired suddenly means nothing. In the game of life, we sometimes land on the wrong square. It's déjà vu. Suddenly we're 10 years old sitting at the kitchen table reading a card with a familiar but unpleasant message: **"Go to jail. Go directly to jail. Do not pass go. Do not collect $200."** But this is not a game, and we are not 10-year-olds.

Solomon put it more eloquently, "The race is not to the swift or the battle to the strong, nor does food come to the wise or wealth to the brilliant or favor to the learned; but time and chance happen to them all. Moreover, no man knows when his hour will come: As fish are caught in a cruel net, or birds are taken in a snare, so men are trapped by evil times that fall unexpectedly upon them" (Ecclesiastes 9:11–12). Life is unpredictable. Whenever inevitable change occurs, life starts over. And starting over is never easy. No one can foresee the shape change will take. It may appear friendly at first—a new way of doing things at work, the impact of a child leaving home, or the effects of advancing years—but even friendly and predictable changes create their share of hardships. And not every change is either predictable or friendly. Change comes in ugly forms too: a debilitating accident, an incurable disease, job loss, the death of a child, a destructive fire, or an unexpected divorce. Solomon was right: As *fish are caught in a cruel net, or birds are taken in a snare, so men are trapped by evil times that fall unexpectedly upon them.*

Why People Resist the Inevitable

If change is inevitable and happens to us all, why don't we just get used to it? Why do sensible people continue to resist inevitable change?

Change has always been a threat to anyone with an investment in the former way of doing things. Just ask the first martyr of Christianity. What was the accusation made against Stephen just before they stoned him? "We have heard him say that this Jesus of Nazareth will destroy this place and *change the customs* Moses handed down to us (Acts 6:14, emphasis added). It was easier to murder Stephen than to accept the changes that acceptance of Jesus as the Messiah would bring. And people still shoot messengers of change. If your doctor advises you to give up smoking, change your diet, and lose 20 pounds, you can always find another doctor. If your new boss introduces new software, requires greater accountability, and reins in the expense accounts, you can subtly sabotage her efforts and, if all else fails, find another job.

Even God Requires Change

It's our nature to resist change and associate only with people and leaders who see life as we do. Paul told the young pastor Timothy, "The time will come when men will not put up with sound doctrine. Instead, to suit their own desires, they will gather around them a great number of teachers to say what their itching ears want to hear" (2 Timothy 4:3). God calls us to repent, to change. God doesn't think like we do. As the prophet said, " 'My thoughts are not your thoughts, neither are your ways My ways,' declares the LORD" (Isaiah 55:8). God's way of doing things requires change in people, situations, and life's priorities. I may be perfectly willing to compromise, but God always wants things His way! It is easier to find a preacher who agrees with us than it is to make our lives agreeable to God. And if change for the better is hard to accept, no wonder we have such a hard time accepting change for the worse. We live in a sinful, imperfect world where misfortune and tragedy are commonplace. And Christians aren't spared the difficulties. As Solomon said, "Time and chance happen to them all" (Ecclesiastes 9:11).

Resisting the inevitable may work for a little while, but change is tenacious by nature. In the end, resistance fails and change prevails. Those who go down fighting may hold their ground for a moment, but eventually they *will* go down. This chapter offers an approach to inevitable change that can minimize the pain and maximize the gain of those who must deal with unavoidable life change.

It's Your Decision

The paratroopers were about to make their first jump from a C-130 at 2,000 feet so they all listened carefully as the sergeant explained what to do if the main chute didn't open.

"Snap back immediately into a tight body position," he said. "Then pull the rip cord of your reserve chute and it will open, bringing you safely to the ground." A private two rows ahead stirred nervously and slowly raised his hand. "What's your question, soldier?" the sergeant called out.

"Sergeant, if my main parachute doesn't open, how long do I have to pull my reserve?"

The sergeant looked directly into the young private's eyes and replied with a slight smile, "The rest of your life, soldier. The rest of your life."

When inevitable change occurs in life, you have a choice to make. You can adjust and move on, or not adjust and spend a great deal of energy fighting a lost cause. The decision you make has no bearing on the outcome. Change occurs with or without your permission. The decision you make does, however, have a great impact on your life. You can curse the darkness or turn on a light. How long do you have to decide? The rest of your life, my friend. The rest of your life.

A year ago I was attending a meeting in Los Angeles as a trustee for a national foundation. As a pastor still actively serving a congregation, I make every effort to be in my pulpit each Sunday. It had been a long meeting at the end of a long day following a very long week. I would be arriving home late Saturday night, just a few short hours before the alarm clock would ring at 5:30 Sunday morning. As I began the long flight home, I turned on my computer and began editing and memorizing my message for the weekend. Half-asleep, I rubbed my eyes to clear away the fog. For some reason the fog didn't lift as I expected. Closing one eye and then the other, I began to realize I couldn't see well enough to read with my left eye. I chalked it up to allergies and did the best I could with my "unaffected" eye. *It'll clear up in a couple of days*, I told myself. When the fog persisted, I decided on a checkup with an ophthalmologist. Three weeks later I was in an examination room looking through a peep hole while Dr. Korn cracked jokes about my profession and discussed the "interesting" and "fascinating" nature of my optical condition.

"I've got good news and better news," he said. "Which do you want to hear first?"

"Make it the good news," I responded.

"Well, the good news is you came to the right place. I know exactly what your problem is."

"What's the better news?" I asked.

"The better news is that I can correct your problem in no time, and maybe even improve your preaching at no extra charge."

"So, what's the problem, Doc?" I asked.

"You have an advanced posterior cataract in your left eye and the same condition in your right eye only less advanced. Fifty years ago your grandfather would have slowly gone blind, but today I can gouge out the old lens, replace it with a new one, and have you seeing again in no time."

I told Dr. Korn I was grateful for his expertise. I admitted I didn't know much about ophthalmology, but as one who worked with words, I recommended that a man in his profession not use the word *gouge* to describe a corrective procedure! That's how quickly a major change came roaring unexpectedly into my life. For more than 40 years I had enjoyed perfect vision. Today I can't read a book, work on my lawnmower, or write a letter without glasses.

I had lots of questions for Dr. Korn: Why did it happen? Will the implants affect other factors in my eye, increase the likelihood of a detached retina or developing glaucoma? Although my doctor was good-natured, well-informed, and optimistic about my prognosis, nothing he said changed the fact that my life was forever changed. In my mind this was *not* a change for the better. It was hard to understand God's purpose in allowing this to happen. I know He doesn't cause all things, but He certainly permits evil to have its way in our less than perfect world. I couldn't help but recall the psalmist's frustration over God's apparent lack of concern:

> *How long, O LORD? Will You forget me forever? How long will You hide Your face from me? How long must I wrestle with my thoughts and every day have sorrow in my heart?*

How long will my enemy triumph over me? Look on me
and answer, O LORD my God. Give light to my eyes,
or I will sleep in death; my enemy will say, "I have over-
come him," and my foes will rejoice when I fall. But I trust
in Your unfailing love; my heart rejoices in Your salvation.
I will sing to the LORD, for He has been good to me.

(Psalm 13)

David was obviously frustrated by a lingering problem that he felt God was ignoring. Despite his frustration, he remained cautiously optimistic about the eventual intervention of the Lord who had helped him so often in the past.

Accepting Unwanted Change

As I experienced this change in my life, I also thought about the stages of grief described by Dr. Elisabeth Kübler-Ross in her classic work *On Death and Dying*. It both amazed and troubled her that medical professionals seemed insensitive to the emotional trauma experienced by those whose condition was beyond the help of their healing arts. Her book helped sensitize the medical world to the needs of the whole person. The five stages of death she documented in her study—denial, rage and anger, bargaining, depression, acceptance[8]—can be traced in anyone experiencing grief over a loss:

1. **Denial**—"This isn't happening to me. I'll wake up and find it's just a dream."
2. **Rage and anger**—"This isn't fair! I did nothing to deserve this!"
3. **Bargaining**—"I'll do whatever you want, God, only make this go away."
4. **Depression**—"Leave me alone. No one understands."

effects of that experience to keep him humble and mindful of his need for God. Just imagine how frustrating poor eyesight would have been on a traveling missionary during the days of Paul. It is troublesome even now to read schedules, catch planes, and decipher street maps.

How did the apostle Paul deal with the effects of unwelcomed change? The key for Paul was faith in Jesus. He knew that God was personally involved in the affairs of people. Jesus didn't sit back in heaven lamenting the sinful condition of the world. He got involved and by His crucifixion restored a sinful people's lost relationship with God His Father. Jesus also got involved directly in Paul's life and stayed involved until the day of Paul's death. Because of God's involvement, Paul approached life with an attitude that kept his problems in perspective.

Did Paul have problems? You better believe it. He once wrote about his troubles by comparing his life to that of the other apostles.

> I have worked much harder, I have been in prison more frequently, been flogged more severely, and been exposed to death again and again. Five times I received from the Jews the forty lashes minus one. Three times I was beaten with rods, once I was stoned, three times I was shipwrecked, I spent a night and a day in the open sea, I have been constantly on the move. I have been in danger from rivers, in danger from bandits, in danger from my own countrymen, in danger from Gentiles; in danger in the city, in danger in the country, in danger at sea; and in danger from false brothers. I have labored and toiled and have often gone without sleep; I have known hunger and thirst and have often gone without food; I have been cold and naked. Besides everything else, I face daily the pressure of my concern for all the churches.   (2 Corinthians 11:23–28)

How did Paul keep his troubles from overwhelming him? The formula is simple but profound. "Do not be anxious about anything, but in everything, by prayer and petition, with thanksgiving, present your requests to God. And the peace of God, which transcends all understanding, will guard your hearts and your minds in Christ Jesus" (Philippians 4:6–7).

The Greek root word for anxious is *mer-os*. Our English word *morose* has the same meaning. We define *morose* as the state of depression or melancholy, but its original definition had a more significant meaning. To be *anxious* or *mer-os* literally meant "to separate or isolate." When we separate or isolate a problem from the rest of life we often end up depressed or melancholy. By focusing on our problems and separating them from our blessings, we allow problems (not blessings) to dominate our thinking and rob us of the perspective God urges us to maintain.

Instead of allowing problems to dominate our thinking, Paul said, *In everything, by prayer and petition, with thanksgiving, present your requests to God.* The formula is simple but profound:

1. Don't isolate your problems, making them greater than they are.
2. Consider difficulties only in light of your blessings.
3. Through a prayer that emphasizes thankfulness, let God know your needs.
4. Last, but not least, enjoy the results: *The peace of God, which transcends all understanding, will guard your hearts and your minds in Christ Jesus.*

Gaining objectivity in times of difficulty is an important first step. No problem is unique to you. No problem is too great for God. No problem lasts forever. Problems have their limits but God has none.

Attitude Is Everything

I recently had the privilege of interviewing a Christian woman who had just celebrated her 100th birthday. She is a pillar of strength in a local residential care facility. She lives alone in an efficiency apartment but ventures out daily to encourage residents, lead a Bible study, or join others in prayer for those who need intercession. She's been a widow for almost 40 years and watched helplessly as her daughter succumbed to cancer. Even these hardships have not diminished Frieda's optimism. The day I stopped for a visit she was preparing a devotional for a Christian women's gathering. I asked how she managed to remain so positive despite all the adversity of her life and the tendency of some to become pessimistic as they grow older. She offered two reasons.

First, Frieda looked beyond the difficulty. She readily admitted that she had suffered her share of disappointments. (Her husband had been badly hurt on the job, which required Frieda to go back to work and provide for their family.) Nevertheless, she described their life as "a good one," and their sorrows as "stepping-stones to greater blessings." Frieda said her cup was always overflowing: "Whenever we encountered a hardship we always wondered how God was going to use it for our good." She even said she felt sorry for those who had it easy. "They have been cheated out of life," she thought. "They have never known the joy of struggle, difficulty, sorrow, and challenge."

Second, Frieda chose her friends carefully. She admitted many people near life's end become negative and cynical about things. "I've never been a part of the critical bunch in any church. I just don't believe in it. The key to joy is doing something for others. I know there are gossips in every church," she said, "but I've never made it my business to get to know them."

Life is an uncertain journey. There are aspects of life that with God's help we can and should change. There are also people and situations in life beyond our ability to change. Inevitable changes and hardships that no one can predict will require acceptance and adaptation. Seeing life from God's perspective can help you weather the storms of unavoidable change. Paul called the ability to be content in good times and bad times, "a secret" (Philippians 4:12). It's a secret Paul shared—the secret to serenity.

Taking Time for Reflection and Personal Growth

Be still, and know that I am God. Psalm 46:10

1. Read Solomon's observation in Ecclesiastes 9:11–12.
   - Suggest a reason why Christians are not spared troubles despite their faithfulness.
   - How is Solomon's observation related to Frieda's attitude?
2. Read Paul's advice to the Philippians in chapter 4:5–13.
   - Why are we told not to be anxious?
3. Why are Dr. Elisabeth Kübler-Ross' five stages of grief so applicable to accepting inevitable, unwanted change in life?
   - Can you identify which stage you're in regarding a change you can't avoid?
   - How can you apply the direction given in Philippians 4?

Pray about Change You Cannot Avoid

Lord, much of life is beyond my control. I did not choose the circumstance of my birth, and the formative years of my life were determined by others. Even now I must handle situations and people whose activities greatly impact my life but over whom I have very little control. I cannot control others, but I can control how I respond to others. I cannot determine the outcome of every circumstance, but I can reflect Your love and truth in the circumstances of my life. Gracious Lord, help me to see life as an opportunity that is new every morning. Help me to expect Your help, to better understand my role in life, and to use my influence to make a difference in the lives of those around me. Through Jesus Christ. Amen.

The Wisdom to Know the Difference

A Story about Hope and the Search for Wisdom

I first met Lisa through a radio interview she was conducting on the subject of Christian leadership. Lisa co-hosts a syndicated program with her father, Lowell Lundstrom, a lifelong evangelist and the founder of Impact America. Their good friend Bruce Schoeman was co-hosting because of commitments that required Lowell's presence elsewhere. The interview flew by as we encouraged Christians to allow their biblical beliefs to permeate their public lives.

After the program, Bruce and I talked off-air at length about his own son and the need for adult Christians to help young people achieve their God-given potential. Bruce also shared the story of Lisa's traumatic separation and eventual reconciliation with her father as an example of his concern for young Christians. The Lundstroms' story is an important one, especially for those who struggle with feelings of helplessness when facing events beyond their control.

The story of "My Precious Prodigal" (Lowell's nickname for his beloved Lisa) began in April 1957 when Lowell and his wife Connie answered God's call and began an evangelistic ministry that continues to this day. They traveled across America with their young family, started a national radio ministry, and produced prime-time TV specials that were aired in the United States and Canada. It was a family affair in which their children also played musical roles. The pace was incredible, with

Lowell preaching and singing 300 nights a year. When the children weren't performing, they were sleeping in guitar cases offstage.

But all was not right with the Lundstroms' precious daughter Lisa. In an article dedicated to helping others avoid the anguish their family endured, Lowell described the night his world came crashing down.

> I'll never forget the nightmare phone call that shattered my world and nearly destroyed my ministry.
>
> "Reverend Lundstrom," the officer said, "I'd like to meet with you at the police station. Your 17-year-old daughter is scheduled to appear in court for propositioning a vice officer."
>
> My hands were trembling as I put down the receiver— and my whole body numbed as I weaved my way through traffic toward the main precinct station.
>
> My daughter, a prostitute? Impossible!
>
> My wife, Connie, and I had dedicated Lisa to Jesus Christ as a baby. We raised her on Bible stories, gospel songs, and prayer. There must be some mistake! The reality of this hellish nightmare was like getting hit with a cement block in the chest when I read the vice officer's description of her proposition. When I opened the police file and saw her mug shot—my knees nearly buckled and I felt close to fainting.
>
> But this was no mistake. My beautiful, precious daughter was a hooker working in a major Midwestern city. Lisa was in peril and my world, as a father, was in shambles.[10]

Words cannot convey the depth of the hurt, pain, doubt, and suffering that the Lundstrom family, including Lisa, went through during her nine-year plunge into the ugly world of prostitution, pimps, and sexual abuse.

The truth about Lisa devastated her family, shattered her dad's sense of spiritual purpose, and shook the very foundations of the Lundstroms' faith. They read the papers and watched news reports with special interest in stories about female murder victims found naked in railroad yards or whose bodies washed up along some river. Worse than their fears for Lisa's physical welfare, the Lundstroms feared for Lisa's eternal destiny. What had they done wrong? What could they do to rescue Lisa? How could they live one more day with the guilt, parental concern, and overbearing heartache they felt for their precious daughter?

The Lundstroms earnestly sought "the peace of God, which transcends all understanding" (Philippians 4:7). They pleaded for the serenity Jesus promised when He told His disciples, "Peace I leave with you; My peace I give you. I do not give to you as the world gives. Do not let your hearts be troubled and do not be afraid" (John 14:27). It was an illusive peace. Lisa was gone. Lowell recalls, "And, worst of all, I felt God had double-crossed me."[11]

How often must they have prayed, "God, grant me the serenity to accept the things I cannot change, the courage to change the things I can, and the wisdom to know the difference." The Lundstrums never gave up hope. As confused and broken as they were, they ever so weakly held on to the promise that God would neither desert them nor forsake them. Although it seemed impossible to believe, they knew that the Lord cared for Lisa with a love even greater than theirs.

Lisa became more and more aware of the destructive nature of her lifestyle and began to suffer the consequences of her choices. Her health and emotional well-being began to falter. Then one night her greatest fear became reality. Lisa was picked up by a client who turned out to be a serial killer responsible for the deaths of 18 women. He tied Lisa up, fully intending to make her his 19th victim. He began describing in detail how he was going to kill her as he ran cold, sharp knives up and down her body. Lisa cried out to the Lord, pleading for divine intervention. What happened next was a miraculous answer to nine years of parental prayer. Lisa said she suddenly felt the presence of God overpower the evil spirit that possessed her captor. Inexplicably, the man released Lisa and took his own life instead.

Lisa's relief was surpassed only by the joy of her parents, who received her home with open arms. The Lundstroms, more than most, understand the overwhelming joy God must feel over every sinner who repents. They could not help but recall Jesus' wonderful story of the prodigal. The words of the forgiving father took on new meaning. "Let's have a feast and celebrate. For this son of mine was dead and is alive again; he was lost and now is found!" (Luke 15:23–24).

The Wisdom to Make Right Choices

Hindsight, as they say, is 20/20. The Lundstroms had no idea how their nine-year ordeal would end. They had faced hundreds of decisions about their family, their ministry, and their daughter during those long years, anxious months, and wearisome days. Should they attempt to rescue Lisa against her will? Was it best to leave her alone or stay in touch? Should they accept her as she was or take a stand against the sinfulness of her life? Were they even fit for ministry? How can they counsel others when their own household was in shambles? Did God care? If He cared, why didn't He act? Had their preoccupation with Lisa become unhealthy? Had they been fair to their other children? Should they talk openly about Lisa in their ministry or keep it a private matter? If Lisa died, would she be saved? What lesson could they learn from this ongoing nightmare? Wisdom was called for.

In such difficult situations Christians must distinguish between those things they can do and those things they must leave to God. What things can Christians change? What things are beyond our ability to change? How can we know the difference?

The Bible says, "The fear of the LORD is the beginning of wisdom; all who follow His precepts have good understanding. To Him belongs eternal praise" (Psalm 111:10). Those words were first spoken by David. He must have said them often because they were repeated twice by his son Solomon in later writings (Proverbs 1:7 and Proverbs 9:10). And they were more than a catchphrase for Solomon.

One Man's Wise Choice

God had always loved Solomon and had given him the special name *Jedidiah*, which meant "beloved of God." After the death of his father, Solomon made a special attempt to seek God's favor as he undertook the responsibility to run the nation. God honored the special offering Solomon made by appearing to the young king in a dream. The Lord invited Solomon to ask for anything he needed to run the kingdom. His choices were unlimited. Solomon could have asked for great wealth, a powerful army, a long life, good health, or popularity among the people. The influence of his father is seen in his answer.

> *Solomon answered, "You have shown great kindness to Your servant, my father David, because he was faithful to You and righteous and upright in heart. You have continued this great kindness to him and have given him a son to*

sit on his throne this very day. Now, O LORD *my God,*
You have made Your servant king in place of my father
David. But I am only a little child and do not know how to
carry out my duties. Your servant is here among the people
You have chosen, a great people, too numerous to count or
number. So give your servant a discerning heart to govern
Your people and to distinguish between right and wrong.
For who is able to govern this great people of Yours?"

(1 Kings 3:6–9).

The Bible says God was extremely pleased with the request Solomon made. The Lord granted him an intellect so sharp God said, "There will never have been anyone like you, nor will there ever be" (1 Kings 3:12). In addition to Solomon's request (and because he resisted the temptation to act selfishly), God also promised, "Moreover, I will give you what you have not asked for—both riches and honor—so that in your lifetime you will have no equal among kings. And if you walk in My ways and obey My statutes and commands as David your father did, I will give you a long life" (1 Kings 3:13–14).

Solomon was concerned about being a wise king for the people of God. What a contrast to the decision his son, Rehoboam, would make when the time came for the crown to pass to him. Instead of making a wise decision based on what was best for the people, Rehoboam listened to unwise counsel that urged he assert himself and demand the respect, service, and heavy taxes of the people. Under Solomon the kingdom prospered. Under the selfish leadership of Solomon's son, the kingdom of Israel divided. The key to true wisdom is obedience to the will of the Lord.

When It's Time to Decide

We can learn a great deal about making wise decisions from Scripture. When a situation calls upon us to either step up or stand down, the following 10 points may help.

Do

1. Hold on to the promises of God.
2. Pray and ask others to pray about the situation.
3. Be still and listen to God and others who can be objective about your problem.
4. Do what you can.
5. Continue to trust God to love and support you.

Don't

1. Waste time looking for someone to blame.
2. Knowingly compromise any part of God's Word.
3. Allow the situation to preoccupy your thoughts.
4. Hide the problem from others.
5. Give up.

Let's look at those suggestions more closely.

Attitudes and Behaviors to Practice in Times of Decision

1. **Hold on to the promises of God.** In the top drawer of my study desk is the book *Precious Bible Promises*. It's filled with the positive promises of God on various topics. The topics run the gamut from basic spiritual issues such as salvation, spiritual growth, prayer, and forgiveness to more practical topics such as promises for times of loneliness, fear, guilt, temptation, sickness, or financial stress. I find this book

quite helpful. You could make a list of your own Bible promises about a subject of special interest to you. Simply take a topic such as "When Treated Unfairly" and begin making a search of all Scriptures that may provide direction on that topic. Ask some of your Christian friends to help. Your list might look like this:

When Treated Unfairly

- Psalm 30:5—"His favor lasts a lifetime; weeping may remain for a night, but rejoicing comes in the morning."

- Psalm 37:7–9—"Be still before the LORD and wait patiently for Him; do not fret when men succeed in their ways, when they carry out their wicked schemes. Refrain from anger and turn from wrath; do not fret—it leads only to evil. For evil men will be cut off, but those who hope in the LORD will inherit the land."

- Psalm 50:15—"Call upon Me in the day of trouble; I will deliver you, and you will honor Me."

- Proverbs 18:10—"The name of the LORD is a strong tower; the righteous run to it and are safe."

- Romans 5:3–5—"We also rejoice in our sufferings, because we know that suffering produces perseverance; perseverance, character; and character, hope. And hope does not disappoint us, because God has poured out His love into our hearts by the Holy Spirit, whom He has given us."

- Romans 12:19—"Do not take revenge, my friends, but leave room for God's wrath, for it is written: 'It is Mine to avenge; I will repay,' says the Lord."

- Romans 12:21—"Do not be overcome by evil, but overcome evil with good."

- 1 Peter 3:13–17—"Who is going to harm you if you are eager to do good? But even if you should suffer for what is right, you are blessed. 'Do not fear what they fear; do not be frightened.' But in your hearts set apart Christ as Lord. Always be prepared to give an answer to everyone who asks you to give the reason for the hope that you have. But do this with gentleness and respect, keeping a clear conscience, so that those who speak maliciously against your good behavior in Christ may be ashamed of their slander. It is better, if it is God's will, to suffer for doing good than for doing evil."

- 1 Peter 5:6–7—"Humble yourselves, therefore, under God's mighty hand, that He may lift you up in due time. Cast all your anxiety on Him because He cares for you."

- Hebrews 12:2–3—"Let us fix our eyes on Jesus, the author and perfecter of our faith, who for the joy set before Him endured the cross, scorning its shame, and sat down at the right hand of the throne of God. Consider Him who endured such opposition from sinful men, so that you will not grow weary and lose heart."

2. **Remember to pray and ask others to pray about the situation.** Through prayer, God changes things and people—don't underestimate Him. In the book of James we are reminded, "Elijah was a man just like us. He prayed earnestly that it would not rain, and it did not rain on the land for three and a half years. Again he prayed, and the heavens gave rain, and the earth produced its crops" (James 5:17–18). The key phrase in that passage is, *was a man just like us.* It is God who gives prayer its power. It is God who knows the best solution to every situation.

3. **Be still and listen.** The world strives for independence but Christians are strongest when they are totally dependent

on the Lord (see Psalm 46:10 and 2 Corinthians 12:10). God didn't make Paul strong to overcome his weakness; in Paul's weakness God's power was made strong.

4. **Do what you can.** Don't allow an unresolved difficulty to paralyze your ability to accomplish daily routines. In difficulty, more than ever, you need the affirmation that comes from accomplishment. Lowell Lundstrom advises parents of prodigals, "Don't spend all your time lamenting your son or daughter's prodigal lifestyle. Get busy helping the youth in your own area."[12]

5. **Continue to trust God to love and support you.** If you could resolve every situation on your own, you would have no need for prayer or trust in the Lord. Of course you would still need the forgiveness that leads to eternal life, but your entire earthly experience would deny rather than reinforce that relationship. The Lord uses life's difficulties to keep His children close and to strengthen the bond of trust. Instead of lamenting difficulty, James suggests a different spirit:

> *Consider it pure joy, my brothers, whenever you face trials of many kinds, because you know that the testing of your faith develops perseverance. Perseverance must finish its work so that you may be mature and complete, not lacking anything. If any of you lacks wisdom, he should ask God, who gives generously to all without finding fault, and it will be given to him. But when he asks, he must believe and not doubt, because he who doubts is like a wave of the sea, blown and tossed by the wind. That man should not think he will receive anything from the Lord; he is a double-minded man, unstable in all he does.*   (James 1:2–8)

God uses difficult times to develop perseverance and faith, leading to maturity and wisdom. When difficult times descend, fall to your knees, thanking God for the opportunity to exercise faith and trust in His provision. Difficult times provide the best opportunity you have to make a powerful witness to nonbelieving friends and family.

Attitudes and Behaviors to Avoid in Times of Decision

1. **Don't waste time looking for someone to blame.** Every Monday morning our staff meets to discuss the previous week's activities and review our calendars for the upcoming two weeks. Everyone—including secretaries and custodians—gathers to debrief as we share the joys and frustrations of our mutual work. If the sanctuary sound system malfunctioned or two meetings were scheduled for the same room at the same time, we make note of it. A corrective action is decided and we move on. A spirit of accusation is never permitted, but a candid discussion of problems is always encouraged. We gather to fix problems not blame. By maintaining a problem-solving attitude we have developed a "can-do" spirit of cooperation and a commitment to excellence. Focusing on past failure is not only a waste of time, it's an unproductive distraction that only prolongs the difficulty.

   The temptation to place blame is greatest when someone else is responsible for a difficulty you must endure. Forgiveness is required by God for this very reason. You can go through life justifying and explaining your limited accomplishments because this person or that situation kept you from being productive. You may even be right, but your life will still be unproductive. God doesn't ask you to forgive others because they deserve it or because it is good for them. We forgive others because God has always forgiven us and because bitterness and resentment are the most destructive attitudes known to man. By not forgiving others we empower them to exert continued control over our lives, which limits our present and future accomplishments.

2. **Don't knowingly compromise any part of God's Word.** The best solution to any difficulty will never require unfaithfulness to the Lord. King Saul's crown wasn't taken away and given to David because Saul lacked courage or leadership ability. Neither is there any indication that his son Jonathan was incapable of assuming leadership of God's people. King Saul lost his throne because he continually compromised God's Word. He did what seemed reasonable rather than submit to God in complete obedience.

Saul once took matters into his own hands rather than wait as instructed for the blessing of the prophet. Later, when God commanded complete destruction of all spoils after a certain battle, Saul brought the best back for bragging rights. When confronted by the prophet, Saul excused his behavior by claiming he disobeyed in order to offer a great sacrifice to God. The prophet's words to Saul should be memorized by anyone tempted to believe the solution to a given difficulty might require disobedience to God: "Samuel replied, 'Does the LORD delight in burnt offerings and sacrifices as much as in obeying the voice of the LORD? To obey is better than sacrifice, and to heed is better than the fat of rams' " (1 Samuel 15:22). The greatest blessing of difficulty is the opportunity to develop greater faith. It should not surprise us that Satan would tempt us with solutions urging compromise of God's Word. Your long-term relationship with God is more critical to success than any short-term solution to a pressing immediate problem. *To obey is better than sacrifice.*

3. **Don't allow the situation to preoccupy your thoughts.**
Remember the lesson of chapter 3: Start by gaining a better perspective. When Paul told the Philippian Christians,
"Do not be anxious about anything" (Philippians 4:6) he
was telling them not to allow any situation to dominate
their thinking and rob them of the perspective God wanted
them to maintain.

One of the best ways I've found to keep an unresolved
situation from dominating my thoughts while keeping up
with daily activities involves a simple two-step procedure.
First, I offer a prayer that God would lead me to know His
will about the situation. Then I write a one- or two-word
description of the problem at the top of a clean page in
the back of my date book. (If you don't have a planning
calendar you can use a spiral notebook small enough to fit
in your purse or pocket.) As I go about my work, ideas
about the unresolved situation naturally occur, so I write
them down on the designated page. This provides an out-
let for ideas and thoughts that may come as an answer to
prayer but keeps me from turning it over and over in my
mind. At the end of the day, or when time allows, I can
choose to reconsider the issue with the help of my written
notes. I'm amazed at how often a word from a daily devotional, the lyrics of Christian song on the radio, or the
observation of an unrelated incident is used by God to
direct my path.

4. **Don't hide the problem from others.** The Bible says, "As
iron sharpens iron, so one man sharpens another"
(Proverbs 27:17). As a somewhat public figure, I am not
inclined to share my struggles with many people, but I do
find it helpful to share a difficult decision with a few close
friends. My wife, Carol, is also an important God-given balance in my life. She approaches problem solving with a dif-

ferent set of skills than I do. She breaks a problem down into its smallest parts and considers the consequence of each alternative. I tend to think only of what is "best" or "right" with little or no thought of consequence. The different perspective and insight she offers can help me reach an important decision.

It should come as no surprise that every 12-step recovery program for addictive personalities requires self-disclosure. Telling someone else about a problem or difficult decision is a very freeing experience. It not only provides an opportunity for fresh insight, it brings objectivity to the issue. As long as the difficulty is a private struggle, we are inclined to think of it as a personal problem. As soon as we share our struggle with another person, the issue itself (not our personal welfare) becomes the focus of attention. Isolation is one of the first signs of a friend in trouble. Satan loves to pick off the stragglers. Times of struggle are no time to be alone. The Bible says, "A friend loves at all times, and a brother is born for adversity" (Proverbs 17:17).

During our year of seminary internship under the direction of a gifted pastor in Minnesota, Carol and I went through a very difficult time. Our first child was born a twin whose brother died at birth. Joshua remained in intensive care for weeks, and Carol was diagnosed with cancer. It was a difficult time fraught with difficult decisions. I grew tired of everyone's interest in our trouble and remember the advice of our pastor. "Stephen," he said, "there is a ministry in allowing others to minister to you." We are created to live in relationships with other people. God intends people to receive and offer assistance to each other: "It is not good for man to be alone" (Genesis 2:18). That is especially true when facing a difficult decision. Solomon was right when he said, "Plans fail for lack of counsel, but with many advisers they succeed" (Proverbs 15:22).

5. **Don't give up.** The shortest speech Sir Winston Churchill ever made was a commencement address. The headmaster of his old school at Harrow prevailed on him to honor the graduates with a few words of wisdom. The hall was understandably filled to capacity. The young boys were told to come prepared to take notes and listen with great attention. Churchill, after all, was the greatest orator of his day, perhaps of his century. After a prolonged applause following his introduction, Churchill allowed complete silence to fall on the room before he spoke. "Never, never, never give up!" After just five words he ended his speech and took his seat. Many a successful person has memorized and heeded his advice.

The apostle told the wavering Christians at Galatia, "Let us not become weary in doing good, for at the proper time we will reap a harvest if we do not give up" (Galatians 6:9). Often the only difference between those who ultimately succeed and those who fail is the number of times they get up after failing.

We are prone to failure because we focus too much on the destination and not enough on the journey. The greatest value of most people's lives is not what the person accomplished but the attitude he or she displayed along the way. If our main purpose in life is to give honor to God and reach lost people with the Gospel of Jesus Christ, there is no special advantage in holding a high position or achieving some great honor. The way we live each day— not the accomplishments of each day—provides the opportunity.

Taking Time for Reflection and Personal Growth

Be still, and know that I am God. Psalm 46:10

1. Read again God's explanation of wisdom in Psalm 111:10.
   * How could this explanation of wisdom help you?
2. Why is it so important to use God's Word when seeking wisdom?
   * Where do you most need to seek wisdom in your life?
   * Use a Bible concordance to make a list of Bible passages that help you apply God's Word to a difficult situation in your life.
3. Name a difficult situation in your life.
   * List things to be thankful for in that situation.
   * What can you learn about the importance of difficulties in life?

Pray for Wisdom When Making Decisions

Gracious Lord, You are the way, the truth, and the life. Fill me with Your wisdom. Give me the water of life to quench my spiritual thirst and the bread of heaven to satisfy my deepest hunger. Lord, today I simply open my heart in search of Your wisdom. Give me greater faith to accept Your direction in my life. By Your Holy Spirit, impart the fruit of faith in my life: love, joy, peace, patience, kindness, goodness, faithfulness, gentleness, and self-control. Overcome my doubts and strengthen my faith for Jesus' sake. Amen.

Part 2

Ten Biblical Principles of Change

Principle 1

Everything Changes except God

Time has a way of changing things—that's for sure. Carol and I recently celebrated her dad's 77th birthday by flying down to the Gulf Coast where he lives. God has blessed Don with good health and an active life—he still volunteers almost daily as a tour guide on the aircraft carrier USS *Lexington*, now a floating naval museum. More than 50 years ago he stood at attention on her flight deck as "Dug-Out-Doug" (his name for General Douglas MacArthur) and the emperor of Japan signed the terms of surrender aboard the Battleship *Missouri* in Tokyo Harbor. It meant the end of World War II, a day Don will never forget.

The *Lexington* and the *Missouri* were once active battleships; now they are reminders of a nation's history. Just look around you for other things that have changed in the last 50 years: answering machines, computers, VCRs, the value of a dollar, the divorce rate, the crime rate, fashions, medicine, etc. Time changes almost everything—even the surface of the earth changes with time.

But God doesn't change. He alone is the stable force around which the whole universe revolves. The oldest psalm in the Bible helps keep it all in perspective. Moses wrote,

> **Lord, you have been our dwelling place** throughout all generations. **Before the mountains were born or You brought forth the earth and the world, from everlasting**

to everlasting You are God. You turn men back to dust,
saying, "Return to dust, O sons of men." For a thousand
years in your sight are like a day that has just gone by,
or like a watch in the night.

(Psalm 90:1–4, emphasis added)

A thousand years (an entire millennium!) in God's sight are like a few hours to us. God always has been and always will be. He has seen it all, heard it all, and knows it all. David said, "From heaven the LORD looks down and sees all mankind; from His dwelling place He watches all who live on earth—He who forms the hearts of all, who considers everything they do" (Psalm 33:13–15).

In the Old Testament each succeeding generation referred to God as the God of their fathers. When Jacob was worried about potential trouble with his estranged brother, Esau, he prayed, "O God of my father Abraham, God of my father Isaac" (Genesis 32:9). Later, when God appeared to Moses at the burning bush, He identified Himself by saying, "I am the God of your father, the God of Abraham, the God of Isaac and the God of Jacob" (Exodus 3:6). Jesus assured us that the dead who die in the Lord still live by saying, "Have you not read what God said to you, 'I am the God of Abraham, the God of Isaac, and the God of Jacob'? He is not the God of the dead but of the living" (Matthew 22:31–32).

By identifying God as the same God that Abraham, Isaac, and Jacob knew and trusted, the present generation was saying that when it comes to God, nothing has changed. God lavished blessings on Abraham; He does the same for us. The concern God had for Isaac is the same concern He has for us. The way He watched over Jacob and all his children is the same way God watches over me and my family and you and yours. There is great comfort in the lessons of the past as long as we know that the God of the past is the God of the present. The writer of the letter to the Hebrews used the same approach to comfort the Jewish people of his day:

> *God has said, "Never will I leave you; never will I forsake you." So we say with confidence, "The Lord is my helper; I will not be afraid. What can man do to me?" Remember your leaders, who spoke the word of God to you. Consider the outcome of their way of life and imitate their faith.* Jesus Christ is the same yesterday and today and forever."
> (*Hebrews 13:5–8, emphasis added*)

God Is Consistent

Ask anyone who has ever played sports the difference between a bad referee and a good referee. The answers will be the same. A good referee is fair to both teams and he is consistent. A bad referee is unpredictable, calling the plays differently each time. An unpredictable referee is by definition unfair. Both the pitcher and the batter want to know if the strike zone is big or small, high or low, inside or outside. They each may have a personal preference, but as long as the umpire is consistent, they know what they have to do. An umpire who calls a low pitch a strike one minute and a moment later calls the same pitch a ball will have both the pitcher and the batter upset with him. How can they know what to throw or when to swing if they don't know the location of the strike zone?

The same is true for basketball. If the referees call a hand-check foul for bumping another player one minute, but allow elbowing and shoving the next, tempers are sure to erupt on the issue of fairness. Some refs call the game close, others let the players play, allowing a lot of rough contact. Good players can accept either condition, but they want the referee to be consistent. They want the calls to be the same on both ends of the floor and from one play to the next. It is important that those in a position of authority be consistent.

With God there is no doubt—He *is* consistent. Saul, the first king of Israel, began his reign as a humble and dedicated servant of God. Unfortunately, wealth and power changed him. Finally, God could take no more and sent the prophet Samuel to tell Saul his days were numbered and the kingdom would be given to another. The reason God gave for His decision was consistency. Saul's actions were hypocritical, something God will never be. "Samuel said to him, 'The LORD has torn the kingdom of Israel from you today and has given it to one of your neighbors—to one better than you. He who is the Glory of Israel *does not lie or change* His *mind*; for He is not a man, that He should change His mind' " (1 Samuel 15:28–29, emphasis added).

One of the best places to see God's consistency in action is in the Bible. We often treat Bible accounts as mere stories; but they are so much more than trivial facts about people dead and buried. They are a living witness to the way God acts and interacts with His people. God has not changed. The same God who led Abraham out of Haran and Moses across the Sinai is the God who leads His people through life to life eternal.

The story of David shows how God supports those whose hearts are committed to His will. Through David's sinfulness, we see the forgiveness and restoration of God. In the life of Hezekiah, we see how God answers prayer. And in the life of Elijah, we learn it is more important to be faithful than to stand with the majority or the powerful. The God of these Bible "stories" is the God of today. We can learn from His interactions with His people and from the laws of the Old Testament.

Old Testament Civil Laws

There are three different kinds of law found in the Old Testament: civil, ceremonial, and moral. The civil (or political) laws governed people's behavior as a society. For example, Israelites could borrow money from and loan money to each other but they could not charge interest. If a person became seriously indebted, he and his family could be required to work for the one to whom they were indebted, but they could not be treated as slaves. Land could be sold but it would not pass hands forever. Every 50th year the nation celebrated a "Year of Jubilee" when all debts were forgiven and lands were returned to the family of origin. Of course, there were also many other laws about this or that offense and appropriate consequence for illegal activity.

Old Testament Ceremonial Laws

The ceremonial laws of Israel governed the worship practices of the nation. All Israelites, including the priests, were required to tithe from the first and the best of all they received. Even firstborn children had to be "redeemed" with an offering to remind the parents that the first of everything belongs to God. Three times a year every man was required to "appear before the Lord" in Jerusalem on behalf of his family. Required appearances at the temple included the celebration of Passover, the Feast of Pentecost (also called Firstfruits), and the Feast of Booths (also called the Feast of Harvest). The Sabbath was considered holy to the Lord. No work could be done on the Sabbath, not even by servants or animals of burden. The priests were required to burn incense in the temple every morning and every evening when they trimmed the perpetually burning lamps in front of the Holy of Holies. Certain offerings were prescribed for various activities as well.

Old Testament Moral Laws

The moral laws of the Old Testament were summarized in the Ten Commandments, which God first gave to Moses on Mount Sinai (see Exodus 20). Later, Moses repeated these commandments in the book of Deuteronomy, which means "the second giving of the law" (see Deuteronomy 5). Not all Christians number them the same way but all agree that they are found in Exodus 20 and Deuteronomy 5. God's commandments require that we do the following:

1. Have no God but the true God.
2. Honor God through the proper use of His name.
3. Worship God in sincerity and truth.
4. Honor and respect those in God-given authority over us, beginning with our parents.
5. Refrain from activity that would hurt or harm our neighbor.
6. Maintain sexual purity before and during marriage.
7. Neither steal from nor defraud our neighbor of his possessions.
8. Avoid gossip and destructive talk about others.
9. Never covet our neighbor's possessions.
10. Never covet our neighbor's relationships.

Which Laws Apply?

Christians today are not bound by the Old Testament civil laws. As times have changed, so have governments. While our civil laws are much different than those of the Old Testament, the Bible tells us clearly that we are to obey current civil laws: "Everyone must submit himself to the governing authorities, for there is no authority except that which God has established. The authorities that exist have been established by

God" (Romans 13:1). The exception is when our governing authorities pass laws that violate God's law. In those instances, we are to obey God's law (see Acts 5:29).

We are also no longer bound by Old Testament ceremonial law. When Jesus came as Messiah, the purpose of the ceremonial law was fulfilled: "Do not let anyone judge you by what you eat or drink, or with regard to a religious festival, a New Moon celebration or a Sabbath day. These are a shadow of the things that were to come; the reality, however, is found in Christ" (Colossians 2:16–17).

We *are*, however, bound by Old Testament moral law, namely the Ten Commandments. God made us and knows what is best for us. He has established His standards for our benefit. He told Israel, "I am setting before you today a blessing and a curse—the blessing if you obey the commands of the LORD your God that I am giving you today; the curse if you disobey the commands of the LORD your God and turn from the way that I command you today" (Deuteronomy 11:26–28). (See also Deuteronomy 28.)

When facing changes and making decisions about life, it is important for us to know that God's standards for our behavior are the same today as they were at creation and when He gave Moses the Ten Commandments. God established His moral standards for our benefit, not for our frustration. He knows how relationships are best established and what kinds of activities destroy.

Because we are forgiven by God through faith in Jesus, we are not troubled by guilt over past sins, but our present and our future are directed by those standards that will be most beneficial for us and for others. The Bible says, " 'Everything is permissible'—but not everything is beneficial. 'Everything is permissible'—but not everything is constructive. Nobody should seek his own good, but the good of others" (1 Corinthians 10:23–24).

Divine Principles

Because God's moral standards are the same today as they have always been, divine principles also remain the same. God's principles for raising children, maintaining a marriage, leading people, conducting business, and problem solving are as applicable today as they were for Abraham, Isaac, and Jacob.

We can study the account of Eli's faithfulness to God and of his failure to discipline his sons and learn that parental godliness is no guarantee that our children will grow up godly. We can examine the life of David and be reminded that even those closest to God are subject to temptations that can destroy them, their families, and others. David's life also shows how God's compassion is extended to the fallen and how He restores those who repent of their sins.

Because God has not changed, and this world is established on His truth, the Bible becomes a rich resource of divine help for our lives.

In the New Testament Paul said, "All Scripture is God-breathed and is useful for teaching, rebuking, correcting and training in righteousness, so that the man of God may be thoroughly equipped for every good work" (2 Timothy 3:16–17). David discovered the same great value in God's Word a thousand years earlier when he wrote of it in Psalm 119, the longest chapter in the Bible. God's truth gave David a huge advantage in life.

Oh, how I love your law! I meditate on it all day long.
Your commands make me wiser than my enemies,

for they are ever with me. I have more insight than all my teachers, *for I meditate on your statutes. I have* more understanding than the elders, *for I obey Your precepts. I have kept my feet from every evil path so that I might obey Your word. I have not departed from Your laws, for You Yourself have taught me. How sweet are Your words to my taste, sweeter than honey to my mouth!*
(Psalm 119:97–103, *emphasis added*)

God's Word Is Common Ground

Another important value of God's changeless nature is the common ground He provides. God's Word provides strength for marriage, unifies families, and links generation after generation to a common heritage.

People are not the same—just ask anyone who has ever parented more than one child. When Carol and I first met, we had a lot of things in common. We went to the same college, ate in the same cafeteria, knew the same people, took some of the same classes, and enjoyed a life that was very similar. Today, there is little about our lives that is the same. Preschool children surround her from 8:00 until 3:15 every day. She ties shoes, soothes scrapes, stretches imaginations, and directs developmental activities that teach socialization, logic, and discovery. She eats at a table so low and in chairs so small I need special assistance getting up and down every time I stop to see her! It is easy to see how couples who had so much in common when they first met discover they have little in common 10 or 20 years later. No wonder people are divorcing and remarrying different people for each phase of life. Our marriage might be the same except for one important difference: The most important thing in Carol's life and the most important thing in my life is always the same. No matter how different our daily activities have become, we walk on the common ground of God's Word and our love for our Savior.

Knowing that God never changes and that His truth is the same yesterday, today, and tomorrow adds stability to life and helps us make wise decisions. Because God is stable, we enjoy stability. Stability is an important first step in achieving serenity. It is the first of 10 principles that will change your life.

Serenity Principle 1: Everything Changes except God

Putting Principle 1 into Action

1. God's love is constant. But how does that apply directly to your life? Read God's description of love recorded in 1 Corinthians 13.
   - Make a list of the attributes of true love.
   - Next to each item on your list, write a way God has demonstrated that attribute in your life.
   - Use this list as a reminder that even though your life and circumstances will change, God's love doesn't— He loves you yesterday, today, and tomorrow.
2. Mary's praise of God for the good news of Jesus' coming birth is a classic description of the unchangeable nature of God. Read Luke 1:46–55 to review the reasons Mary gave for singing God's praise.
   - Make a list of reasons *you* sing God's praise.
   - Do any of those reasons relate to His stability?
3. As you encounter change in your life (minor or major) write it down in a prayer journal. Continue to pray about the changes in your life.

- When God has answered your prayer, write down His answer and how it affected you.
- After a few months, look back to the beginning of your journal to see God's constant love in your life.

Pray about the Unchangeable Nature of God

Dear God of Abraham, Isaac, and Jacob, hear my prayer and bless my life with the peace that only You can give. I am honored by Your love and humbled by Your concern. Thank You for the consistent love You have demonstrated in every generation. Thank You also for the standards on which You have established Your world. As I study the stories and the lessons of the Bible, open my heart to understand and accept Your truth. Send Your Holy Spirit to help me withstand times of temptation. Give me peace, Lord, and let others experience Your love and acceptance through me. Grant it for Jesus' sake. Amen.

Principle 2

Expect Opposition

Someone once said, "If you want to make enemies, change something." No truer words were ever spoken. The denomination of my childhood is a wonderful, Christ-centered, and hardworking family of Christian people. They love their Lord and they love their church. They are a people steeped in a history, heritage, and culture developed over 500 years. Those beliefs and traditions have been passed from generation to generation since the time of Martin Luther. Understandably, Lutherans are fiercely proud of their beliefs and traditions, which can make it very hard for them to accept change.

The hymnal of my childhood was published in 1941. Like most every other child born and raised in the Lutheran church, I knew my hymnal inside and out. Most of us were given our own special copy with our name engraved on it when we were confirmed on Palm Sunday at age 13. Those old hymnals were bound in either blue or red covers. When I graduated from the seminary I was given a black clergy edition, which I must say immediately became one of my prized possessions. That was in 1978. You can imagine the adjustment that was required when, in 1982, our denominational headquarters decided it was time to publish a *new* hymnal with *new* liturgical settings and *new* hymn selections. That transition proved to be a wonderful learning experience for a young and inexperienced pastor like me.

Not everyone was quick to embrace the change. I remember reading a letter on the editorial page of a popular Lutheran newspaper that had been critical of the new hymnal. It asked for copies of all the articles the paper had published opposing the new hymnal. The writer of the letter said many people in his congregation also opposed the new hymnal's adoption and they needed to know why. When it comes to change, our answer often is: No. *Just give us a moment and we'll find out why.*

Opposition to change isn't limited to hymnals, styles of worship, Lutherans, or even the Christian church. Resistance to change is common to every condition of life. Just ask any mechanic whose tool box is twice the size it should be because he lives in two different worlds—the one that measures everything in the metric system and the one that uses standard measurements of inches and feet. So what if the rest of the world uses metric measurements? We were not brought up that way and aren't about to change now. Don't talk to us about meters, grams, and liters. Speak American. Tell us in terms we can understand. How long is it in *feet*? How far is it in *miles*? How much does it weigh in *ounces*?

People who make changes can be a threat to those who liked things the way they were, even if a change would obviously improve a given situation. Families who decide to start attending church can make their unchurched friends uncomfortable—not intentionally of course, but uncomfortable just the same. The person who quits drinking endures the ongoing temptation of drinking friends and situations. He must find new ways to socialize that don't include a cold one, the familiar clatter of ice, and the relaxing effect of alcohol. The mom trying to diet may have a car full of children who can't understand why they no longer eat every other meal at McDonald's. And smokers never realize just how often they lit one up until they decide to stop. Suddenly they wonder what nonsmokers do after lunch, during breaks, and while waiting for their children to finish practice. They've been smoking so long it's hard even to concentrate without a cigarette.

If change is good for us, shouldn't it be easy? Wrong things ought to be hard, and right things ought to be easy. Unfortunately, we are no longer living in the Garden of Eden. Sin changed the world and those who lived in it. It didn't take long for the effects to become apparent. After Cain and Abel were fully grown and working on their own, a small problem developed between them. They both had been raised to know the Lord and to honor Him with offerings from the first and the best of their possessions. Abel was a shepherd so he presented offerings from the first and best of his flocks. Cain was a farmer who made offerings from his harvest. The Bible doesn't tell us the exact reason the Lord considered Abel's offering better than Cain's. It does say, "By faith Abel offered God a better sacrifice than Cain did. By faith he was commended as a righteous man, when God spoke well of his offerings" (Hebrews 11:4).

Perhaps Abel offered only his best while Cain offered an inferior part of his crop. Or maybe it was not the quality or quantity of their offerings but the attitudes behind their offerings that made the difference. The Bible says, "Each man should give what he has decided in his heart to give, not reluctantly or under compulsion, for God loves a cheerful giver" (2 Corinthians 9:7). For whatever reason, one brother found favor with God and the other didn't. The solution seems simple enough: Cain would have to change. Nothing Abel was doing was beyond Cain's ability. Out of concern and kindness for Cain, the Lord gave him some advice: "Why are you angry? Why is your face downcast? If you do what is right, will you not be accepted? But if you do not do what is right, sin is crouching at your door; it desires to have you, but you must master it" (Genesis 4:6–7). Cain had another option—different than the one God suggested—and that is what he chose. Rather than deal with his sin, Cain removed the source of his guilt by killing his brother.

Make no mistake about it, change is hard but not impossible. And what God requests, He enables. Jesus gave a thief by the name of Zacchaeus the same opportunity as Cain, but with different results. Zacchaeus made a dramatic turnaround. Not only did he vow to quit cheating his fellow Jews, he promised he would give half of all he had to the poor and return four times the amount stolen to those he had cheated. It was quite a change for one whose life had been devoted to greed and selfishness. Jesus must have smiled when He said, "Today salvation has come to this house, because this man, too, is a son of Abraham. For the Son of Man came to seek and to save what was lost" (Luke 19:9–10). Change is hard but not impossible.

Opposition Can Be Useful

Not all opposition is created equal—some criticism is beneficial. Opposition keeps us honest and forces us to answer tough questions on everything from motives to methods. Solomon understood the value of critics: "Wounds from a friend can be trusted, but an enemy multiplies kisses" (Proverbs 27:6).

The story of Ahab and Jehoshaphat demonstrates the importance of critics: Ahab from the North and Jehoshaphat from the South were deciding if they should go to battle against the city-state Ramoth Gilead. Jehoshaphat (the godly king of Judah) was more than willing to engage in the battle, provided that the Lord gave His blessing through the prophets. "No problem," Ahab replied, and he called for 400 prophets who immediately predicted victory. Jehoshaphat was not impressed. Something about the way the prophets acted convinced him they were only saying what the kings wanted to hear. "Jehoshaphat asked, 'Is there not a prophet of the LORD here whom we can inquire of?' " (1 Kings 22:7).

Ahab made no attempt to dissuade Jehoshaphat from his assessment of the situation. Apparently, the insincerity of the 400 prophets was beyond defending. "There is still one man through whom we can inquire of the LORD, but I hate him because he never prophesies anything good about me, but always bad. He is Micaiah son of Imlah" (1 Kings 22:8). After a mild rebuke from Jehoshaphat, Ahab called for Micaiah to make his pronouncement. The servant sent to bring Micaiah told him that all the prophets were predicting victory, and he urged Micaiah to predict the same. At first Micaiah joined in the praise of the false prophets, evidently mimicking their phony encouragement. His satirical tone must have been obvious. King Ahab replied, "How many times must I make you swear to tell me nothing but the truth in the name of the LORD?" (1 Kings 22:16).

Micaiah's demeanor changed. He became deadly serious and spoke directly to his king. "I saw all Israel scattered on the hills like sheep without a shepherd, and the LORD said, 'These people have no master. Let each one go home in peace' " (1 Kings 22:17). Ahab was furious. He turned to King Jehoshaphat and said, "Didn't I tell you that he never prophesies anything good about me, but only bad?" (1 Kings 22:18). He had the prophet Micaiah thrown into jail and fed only bread and water until the kings' return from the battle. But Micaiah replied, " 'If you ever return safely, the LORD has not spoken through me.' Then he added, 'Mark my words, all you people!' " (1 Kings 22:28). Ahab disguised himself during the battle so that the enemy could not identify him as the king. Nevertheless, as Micaiah had predicted, an enemy archer shot a random arrow that struck Ahab in a joint of his armor, mortally wounding him. He'd have been much better off to listen to his critic.

Critics can be important assets, but not every critic should be given equal time. Follow these suggestions for determining the value of a critic's comments:

1. **What motivates the criticism?** Is it fear, personal dislike for you, or an honest concern about the outcome of your decision?

2. **Is your critic respected by others as a reasonable person whose counsel should be seriously considered?** Know your critic's reputation. If it's not a good one, pay no attention to the criticism.

3. **Does the life of your critic reflect godly qualities?** Review the fruit of the Spirit of which Paul writes in Galatians 5. Is it evident in the person's life?

4. **Does your critic always oppose change or is he objective about each issue as it is offered for consideration?** If the critic is known for opposing any kind of change, he probably isn't very open-minded. Listen to a critic who is objective about the issues he considers.

5. **How will this decision affect your critic?** Does she have something to be gained or lost by virtue of this decision? If so, take the criticism with a grain of salt.

6. **What is the consequence of agreeing or disagreeing with the position your critic has taken?** Carefully weigh the advantages and disadvantageous of each decision.

Honest answers to these questions would have helped

the kings make a better decision about their battle at Ramoth Gilead.

1. Micaiah's motivation was to be honest as a true prophet of God.

2. King Ahab respected Micaiah but resented Micaiah's unwillingness to side with him.

3. There was no question about the godly qualities evident in the life of the prophet.

4. Micaiah was not predictable except in his constant opposition to King Ahab, whose life showed a contempt for justice.

5. The outcome of the battle would have no effect on Micaiah personally.

6. The consequence for King Ahab was a matter of life and death. Obviously, the king's pride cost him his life. Pride still keeps many people from listening to the important and often helpful comments of their critics.

Spiritual Warfare

Carol and I live in the country just outside of St. Louis County, Missouri. Our church is located in a suburban neighborhood 20 minutes away. I grew up in the country and considered life in the woods a helpful counterbalance to the demands of our fast-paced existence. The seven acres on which we built our home was originally part of a farm that was subdivided into 14 lots. Our building site was in the wood-lot, a part of the farm left undeveloped as a source of wood for the homesteader's cookstoves and wood-burning furnaces.

I noticed the trees on our lot were of two distinct types. Half of the site contains huge oaks, hickories, and hard maples. The soil on which they grow is dark and littered with the remains of fallen trees and the loam that rotting leaves and vegetation have produced over many years. The other half is covered with red cedars and honey locusts, which can grow almost anywhere with little or no depth of soil. In Missouri it's not unusual to see a red cedar tree growing from the side of a steep cliff where an errant seed managed to grab a foothold.

A tenacious little vine also inhabits the shallow limestone soil of Missouri. The vine is an insidious little devil that can grow fast enough to cover an entire tree in just one season. No thicker than your little finger, it wraps itself around the trunk of the cedars and honey locusts as it climbs toward the light. The vines, though small, are strong as steel. Trees held in their grasp will yield as the vines constrict their growth and cut into the girth of their trunks. One 60-foot cedar on our lot had its proud top doubled over by the grasp of vines that refused to stretch to accommodate the cedar's growth. We are engaged in mortal combat with the vines. Each spring we mount an all-out campaign to destroy their hold on the trees of our land.

It is an exhausting battle. So long as we stand our ground with hatchet, ax, and bushwhacker, the vines are no match. Huge piles of vines are gathered for burning as the trees bob in appreciation of their release. But while we sleep, and during the wet season when ticks and poison plants protect the thickets from our intrusion, the chopped and beaten vines revive and attempt to reassert their claim on our trees. I asked locals the key to success against such an unrelenting foe. Their answer was biblical: "Watch and pray," they said. "Watch and pray." After years of effort, and the recovery of other less destructive ground cover, the vines will eventually tire and die. We are still waiting.

Watch and pray. Those were the same words Jesus used as

He counseled Peter in the Garden of Gethsemane the night of His arrest. "Watch and pray so that you will not fall into temptation. The spirit is willing, but the body is weak" (Matthew 26:41). As Christians attempt to make progress through change they can expect unrelenting opposition from the devil and his hirelings. So long as we stand in the body armor of the Lord, we are safe and the enemy is defeated. But Satan is patient and always waiting for his next opportunity. Like the vines on my property, he is no match for the sword of the Lord, which is the Word of the God. But also like the vines on my property, he waits for those moments when I am sleeping or threatened by the concerns of life to reassert his subtle but steellike grasp.

For good reason I gave each of my sons a verse to guide and help them in their fight against the deadly and persistent vine—Satan. My oldest son's verse is especially applicable. Paul reminded the Christians at Ephesus they were fighting superior forces when he wrote, "Our struggle is not against flesh and blood, but against the rulers, against the authorities, against the powers of this dark world and against the spiritual forces of evil in the heavenly realms. Therefore put on the full armor of God, so that when the day of evil comes, you may be able to stand your ground, and after you have done everything, to stand" (Ephesians 6:12–13).

We are sinful, not divine. We relax our watch. We fall asleep. The cares and concerns of life distract us from the source of our strength. The devil, like those persistent vines, will be ready to destroy our lives and wreck our homes. The key is remembering that you cannot fight him alone. The rest of Ephesians 6 describes the source of the Christian's confidence:

Stand firm then, with the belt of truth buckled around your

waist, with the breastplate of righteousness in place, and with
your feet fitted with the readiness that comes from the gospel
of peace. In addition to all this, take up the shield of faith, with
which you can extinguish all the flaming arrows of the evil
one. Take the helmet of salvation and the sword of the Spirit,
which is the word of God. And pray in the Spirit on all
occasions with all kinds of prayers and requests. With this in
mind, be alert and always keep on praying for all the saints.
(Ephesians 6:14–18)

Even when you fail, hope is not lost. The Lord is more tenacious than the devil. Jesus said, "I give them eternal life, and they shall never perish; no one can snatch them out of My hand. My Father, who has given them to Me, is greater than all; no one can snatch them out of My Father's hand" (John 10:28–29). The passage assigned to guide our second son, Jacob, is important for Christians whose sinful human nature causes them to stumble. It is from the song of a man who knew all about moral failure and the forgiveness of God. David wrote, "As far as the east is from the west, so far has He removed our transgressions from us. As a father has compassion on his children, so the LORD has compassion on those who fear Him; for He knows how we are formed, He remembers that we are dust" (Psalm 103:12–14).

God knows. He knows *how we are formed*. He is mindful of our weakness and our need for His forgiveness, His renewal, and His strength to face the enemy. The great hymn of Martin Luther reminds us that the final victory is assured by Jesus:

> With might of ours can naught be done,
> Soon were our loss effected;
> But for us fights the valiant One,
> Whom God Himself elected.

Ask ye, Who is this?
Jesus Christ it is, Of sabaoth Lord,
And there's none other God;
He holds the field forever.[13]

Preparing for Opposition

Peter told the Christians that the devil prowled the earth like a lion looking for prey. Expecting opposition is half the battle. He told those Christians to resist Satan by standing firm in their faith, knowing that the opposition they were facing was nothing new and should be expected. Then Peter added this promise, "And the God of all grace, who called you to His eternal glory in Christ, after you have suffered a little while, will Himself restore you and make you strong, firm and steadfast. To Him be the power for ever and ever. Amen" (1 Peter 5:10–11).

Serenity Principle 2 is *Expect Opposition*. God wants Christians to have peace on earth, even if it's the peace found in the eye of a storm. We know that God's peace doesn't guarantee a life free from opposition. In fact, standing with God guarantees the very opposite. We will be assaulted by the enemy on every side but shall not be especially threatened by him. We know he is coming and aren't afraid to fight a battle God has already won. Micaiah told Ahab and Jehoshaphat not to engage in a losing cause. Jesus our Savior says, "Do not be afraid, little flock, for your Father has been pleased to give you the kingdom" (Luke 12:32). That's a promise you can count on, no matter what your opposition.

Serenity Principle 2: Expect Opposition

Putting Principle 2 into Action

1. Read Luke 21:10–19. Why was it important for Jesus to tell His disciples in advance of the coming hardship they would endure?
   - When you face a struggle in your life, do you like to know ahead of time what to expect? Why or why not?
   - Name a struggle in your life. Ask God to help you deal with the hardships it brings. Thank Him for the strength He provides.
2. Read Romans 8:14–25.
   - What help does the Bible offer to those who may undergo a great deal of suffering here on earth?
   - How can the message in Romans help you deal with your struggles?

Pray When You Face Opposition

Lord, You know how cunning Satan can be. You opposed his temptation in the wilderness by standing on Your Father's promises. When I face opposition, help me to remember Your Word. Give me the same assurance You gave Your disciples. Sometimes I can be overwhelmed by the thought of what lies ahead and worry if I will be able to withstand it. Remind me of all that You have done for me and all the faithful—how You closed the mouths of lions, quenched the fires, and put foreign armies to flight by the breath of Your mouth. I am glad that You are not surprised by my failures and won't reject me because of my sins. Your Word gives guidance and peace to my heart. Comfort, keep, and reassure me, Lord, for I seek Your peace through the Prince of Peace, Jesus Christ. Amen.

Principle 3

Know What Is Best, Right, and True

If we don't change the direction we're going, we are likely to end up where we are headed.

—Chinese Proverb

No matter how far you have gone down a wrong road, turn back.

—Turkish Proverb

Have you ever noticed how often life is described in terms of travel?

- We've come to a fork in the road.
- That's when things took a turn for the worse.
- Keep it on the straight and narrow.
- Somewhere along the way, the wheels came off!
- A bend in the road is not the end of your journey, unless you fail to make the turn.

My grandparents lived on a farm just outside of town. On the way to Grandpa Hower's farm, we passed a series of Burma Shave signs. (Burma Shave was a popular shaving cream before the days of electric razors and pressurized cans.) The signs were small, just large enough to contain a short phrase that rhymed with the next one 30 or 40 feet ahead. The last sign in the series always contained the product name: **Burma Shave!** As kids we knew exactly where the signs were located, but Mom would announce their approach anyway and we would read them in unison: Don't lose your head ... to gain a minute ... you need ... your head ... your brains are in it ... **Burma Shave!** It was a great gimmick that helped a struggling company gain international acclaim.

Allen G. Odell was the creator of the idea and its chief promoter. His father owned the Burma-Vita Company but needed to be convinced the campaign was a good idea. He gave Allen $200 for a test. Allen made the first two sets of signs himself and erected them in southern Minnesota along U.S. Highway 61 near Red Wing, and U.S. Highway 65 near Albert Lea. The rest is advertising history. The concept was so well received the sign-making shop became bigger than the shaving cream plant, producing more than 35,000 sets of Burma Shave signs. Farmers vied for the privilege of having the signs posted on their property. Those who did the best job of maintaining them might win a cash award of $500. The signs mixed humor, traffic safety, and sales promotion to create a winning combination. These were some of the all-time favorite slogans:[14]

The whale ... put Jonah ... down the hatch ...
coughed him up! ... because he scratched ...
Burma Shave!

Don't stick ... your elbow ... out too far ...
it might go home ... in another car! ... Burma Shave!

Drinking drivers ... nothing worse ... they put
the quart ... before the hearse ... Burma Shave!

Keep well to the right ... of an oncoming car ...
get your close shaves ... from the half-pound jar ...
Burma Shave!

If these signs blur ... and bounce around ... you'd
better park ... and walk to town ... Burma Shave!

Burma Shave made a business out of helping keep drivers alert and safety conscious. The Bible can serve the same purpose for Christians traveling down life's highway. If God's truth was painted on 36″ signs, mounted atop 8′ posts and placed along the highway, it might read like this:

"I am the way ... the truth, and the life. ... No one comes ... to the Father ... except through Me." ... Jesus Christ! (John 14:6)

"I am the light ... of the world. ... Whoever follows me ... will never walk in darkness ... but will have the light of life." ... Jesus Christ! (John 8:12)

Is Truth Forever True?

Burma Shave signs are no more. They prophesied their own demise when they advertised, "Shaving brushes ... you'll soon see 'em ... on a shelf ... in some museum ... **Burma Shave!**" The signs became victims of a faster pace of life. Words legible at 40 mph along country highways are no longer practical at interstate speeds of 70 mph, set back 150 feet from the road. Many people view the truth of the Bible in the same way. They say biblical truth has run its course, served its purpose. Life is different today. What worked for Dad and Mom just doesn't work anymore.

Has God's Word become irrelevant and archaic? Are the principles and truths of a past generation true for every generation?

Jesus taught that truth did exist. He said it was timeless, and He called it the key to a full and free life. He told His followers, "If you hold to My teaching, you are really My disciples. Then you will know the truth, and the truth will set you free" (John 8:31–32).

President Harry Truman agreed. A great student of history, Truman said in his autobiography, "The only thing new in the world is the history you don't know. And that's true because human nature doesn't change. I sometimes wish it did, but I'm afraid it just isn't possible. At least that's what I've learned from studying history."[15] Times change but people don't. We may drive faster, dress differently, and live with greater convenience, but the issues of greed, dishonesty, jealousy, distrust, and deception still plague our society. Things may look different but people are the same. Not everyone would agree. There have always been people who deny the truth, but denying the truth makes it no less true. Take the presidential election of 1948 for example.

When the incumbent president went to bed on November 2, 1948, everybody except Harry Truman believed New York Governor Thomas E. Dewey would be the next president. Perhaps the most famous of all headline bloopers was printed the next day by the *Chicago Tribune*, "Dewey Defeats Truman." President Truman picked up a copy and posed for the now-famous picture showing just how wrong the "experts" can be. He said, "I tell you, after the election, there was so much crow eaten by the experts, the conservationists thought that the species might disappear from the face of the earth."[16] Truman didn't have much sympathy for such experts or for those they misled. He summarized, "Newspapermen, and they're all a bunch of lazy cusses, once one of them writes something, the others rewrite it and rewrite it, and they keep right on doing it without ever stopping to find out if the first fellow was telling the truth or not."[17]

The popularity of a position in no way determines its truthfulness. Jesus said, "Enter through the narrow gate. For wide is the gate and broad is the road that leads to destruction, and many enter through it. But small is the gate and narrow the road that leads to life, and only a few find it" (Matthew 7:13–14). Holding on to Jesus' teaching (see John 8:31) sets us free to enjoy the life God has given us. His teaching is not a religion of dos and don'ts. It is an understanding that God loves us and, by Jesus' death and resurrection, has rescued us from sin, death, and the devil. The same God who saved us also wants us to have life "to the full" (see John 10:10). We aren't asked to live a certain way to obtain God's favor. Our perfection is secured through forgiveness. We live faithful lives out of gratitude for our rescue, and because the heavenly Father knows what is best for His children. His truth *is* truth, and His way is the best way.

God Is Not Politically Correct— Just Correct

A key to serenity is having the "courage to change the things I can." It stands to reason we must first know what needs changing. Review the Ten Commandments as they appear in Principle 1 (page 92).

The Ten Commandments can be easily divided into two groups, sometimes called the two tables. Jesus summarized them that way when He was asked which were the most important:

> *"The most important one," answered Jesus, "is this:*
> *'Hear, O Israel, the Lord our God, the Lord is one.*
> *Love the Lord your God with all your heart and with*
> *all your soul and with all your mind and with all your*
> *strength.' The second is this: 'Love your neighbor as*
> *yourself.' There is no commandment greater than these."*
> (Mark 12:29–31)

Did you notice the verb Jesus used to describe correct behavior toward God and our neighbor? It was the same in both instances. We are to *love* God. We are to *love* our fellow man. "Love is the fulfillment of the law" (Romans 13:10). The Ten Commandments specifically define how such love is to be demonstrated.

Many decisions are easily reached based on the objective truth of the Ten Commandments or other scriptural teaching. You don't have to search very hard to see that God's truth is not the same as popular opinion:

- On the issue of marriage and divorce, He says, "For this reason a man will leave his father and mother and be united to his wife, and the two will become one flesh. So they are no longer two, but one. Therefore what God has joined together, let man not separate" (Mark 10:7–9).

- On the topic of homosexuality, the Bible says, "Women exchanged natural relations for unnatural ones. In the same way the men also abandoned natural relations with women and were inflamed with lust for one another. Men committed indecent acts with other men, and received in themselves the due penalty for their perversion. ... He gave them over to a depraved mind, to do what ought not to be done" (Romans 1:26–28).

- On the heated issue of abortion and the sacred status of life in the womb, the Bible is crystal clear: "You created my inmost being; You knit me together in my mother's womb. I praise You because I am fearfully and wonderfully made; Your works are wonderful, I know that full well" (Psalm 139:13–14).

These are just a few of the more controversial topics on which the Bible offers commentary. Though centuries old, its content remains amazingly cutting edge. But *knowing* what's right is not always enough. How can we apply God's wisdom to our life? How can we get from where we are to where we want to be? Applying the truth in love is the key to important life change. Paul said, "If I have the gift of prophecy and can fathom all mysteries and all knowledge, and if I have a faith that can move mountains, but have not love, I am nothing" (1 Corinthians 13:2).

Making the Right Decision

Knowing the truth and knowing what is best in a specific situation are not the same thing. Wisdom is the ability to apply biblical truth to the real issues of life. Consider the following as you work to discern God's will in your life.

When Making Decisions

1. **Don't compromise any part of God's Word.** "The end never justifies the means" is trite but true. Remember— God told King Saul, "To obey is better than sacrifice, and to heed is better than the fat of rams" (1 Samuel 15:22).

2. **The answer to your quandary is often obvious but distasteful.** Ask yourself if you are simply avoiding the truth. Given the choice between something difficult or something easy, we are not above choosing the easy way. Some notable prophets had to be rescued from decisions they knew were wrong from the beginning. Jonah was told to go to Nineveh but hopped a ship to Tarshish instead. Abraham made trouble for everyone when he said Sarah was only his sister, not his wife. Peter knew it was hypocritical to eat with Gentiles sometimes but not when prominent Jews were nearby. All three could have saved themselves a lot of trouble if they had done the right thing consistently. Sometimes *knowing* what to do isn't

the hard thing, *doing* it is! James put it more bluntly, "Anyone, then, who knows the good he ought to do and doesn't do it, sins" (James 4:17).

3. **Don't pray answers.** Our church recently concluded a monthlong sermon series on prayer using the well-known acronym ACTS to establish a balanced prayer life: A— Adoration, C—Confession, T—Thanksgiving, and S— Supplication. A colleague was assigned the last message on supplication, which he entitled, "This Isn't Burger King." He told a familiar story of a quick pass by a drive-thru window only to find out down the road that what was in the bag was not what he'd ordered. That common experience can be aggravating. We're tempted to say, "It'll be a long time before I spend good money there again." We often treat prayer the same way. If God doesn't "fill the order," we're inclined to consider the whole business useless activity: "It'll be a long time before I ever pray again!" That's hardly the attitude of Scripture. Even Jesus in the Garden of Gethsemane knew the Father's will—not His own—was best for everyone. John wrote about the great power of prayer, but added the same important condition. "This is the confidence we have in approaching God: that if we ask anything according to His will, He hears us. And if we know that He hears us—whatever we ask—we know that we have what we asked of Him" (1 John 5:14–15). The way we sometimes pray, others might think we are God and He is just our step-and-fetch-it-guy. What a mess we'd make if we got everything we wanted. Picture a 4-year-old filling a shopping cart in a grocery store with everything she ever wanted!

An important part of God's will is for prayer to be unselfish. James wrote, "When you ask, you do not receive, because you ask with wrong motives, that you may spend what you get on your pleasures" (James 4:3). God-pleasing prayer insists on God's will and desires the best outcome for everyone involved. What's best for most doesn't always equate with what's best for me. Mature Christians pray petitions, not answers.

4. **Don't equate faithfulness with success.** God is just as interested in our journey as He is the destination. Faithfulness along the way matters.

5. **Don't equate faithfulness with acceptance**. C. F. W. Walther, a wise pastor who helped found Lutheranism in America, once wrote to young pastors, "Do not be down-hearted because of your controversies! If you could establish your doctrine without such controversies, then it would surely not be the pure Word of God; your controversies are the stocks and bonds … which you hold for the people of the *ecclesia militans* [The Church Militant or the Church on earth]."[18] It was much the same thing that the apostle Paul said when he wrote to the church at Galatia, "Am I now trying to win the approval of men, or of God? Or am I trying to please men? If I were still trying to please men, I would not be a servant of Christ" (Galatians 1:10). Although people tend to know truth when they hear it, it doesn't mean they will accept it, like it, or support it. Don't equate a faithful decision with a popular decision. They are often not the same thing.

6. **Seek the advice of other respected Christians.** Christians seem to be rediscovering the need for accountability. It has always been an important element of personal growth. Solomon told his young students, "As iron sharpens iron, so one man sharpens another" (Proverbs 27:17). He also told them, "Plans fail for lack of counsel, but with many advisers they succeed" (Proverbs 15:22).

The more Christlike we become, the more humble we become. The more humble we become, the more we should seek the advice of mature Christian people. More recent proverbs also apply. One says, "Advice offered when not sought is always perceived as criticism." A second is like it: "When the student is ready, the teacher will appear." Considered together they mean that people typically will not accept advice until they are good and ready to hear it. It is hard to help people whose hearts aren't open to advice. Those seeking help should initiate the conversation.

7. **Admit unconfessed sin.** Unforgiven, unconfessed sin can kill you. It should surprise no one that smack-dab in the middle of a discussion of sickness and health James brings up the subject of confession and forgiveness. In chapter 5 he writes, "Is any one of you sick? He should call the elders of the church to pray over him and anoint him with oil in the name of the Lord. And the prayer offered in faith will make the sick person well; the Lord will raise him up. If he has sinned, he will be forgiven. Therefore confess your sins to each other and pray for each other so that you may be healed" (James 5:14–16).

   Much is written in the Bible about the importance of prayer in the healing process. Christians know that our confidence in prayer comes only through Jesus Christ. He nailed our sin to the cross. When we admit our sin and receive God's forgiveness, we can expect nothing less than His blessing.

8. **Walk by faith, not by sight.** "Faith is being sure of what we hope for and certain of what we do not see. This is what the ancients were commended for. By faith we understand that the universe was formed at God's command, so that

what is seen was not made out of what was visible" (Hebrews 11:1–3). The whole business of creation seems so simplistic, even naive compared to the complex scientific theories of our age. But, as Paul said, "the foolishness of God is wiser than man's wisdom, and the weakness of God is stronger than man's strength" (1 Corinthians 1:25). We accept creation because the One who observed the birth of the universe has proven Himself trustworthy. History, the archaeological record, the fulfillment of ancient prophecies, and the wisdom of God's counsel testify to His trustworthiness.

Christians at their best live by faith, not needing to know outcomes. To know the One who knows the future is enough. His counsel on every issue is sufficient. I have a friend who likes to say, "When in doubt, walk toward the light." Although I contend the phrase is from a movie about poltergeists, it is completely biblical. Jesus is the light of the world. When in doubt, Christians walk in His direction. Life is uncertain and faith doesn't minimize the adventure. Instead, it maximizes the adventure and minimizes the fear. Hand in hand with the Savior, Christians confidently face each new day believing "[nothing] in all creation will be able to separate us from the love of God that is in Christ Jesus our Lord" (Romans 8:39).

9. **Try a number of solutions**. Solomon knew the value of many initiatives. He advised, "Sow your seed in the morning, and at evening let not your hands be idle, for you do not know which will succeed, whether this or that, or whether both will do equally well" (Ecclesiastes 11:6).

Walking by faith is not the same as doing nothing, just waiting for God to take care of you. The Christians at Thessalonica used waiting for the imminent return of

Jesus as an excuse for not working. Paul chided them, "Follow our example. ... we worked night and day laboring and toiling so that we would not be a burden to any of you," and, "If a man will not work, he shall not eat" (2 Thessalonians 3:7–10).

Walking by faith implies that Christians are moving while trusting. Keep moving with your eyes wide open. King David could have demanded the king's throne after Samuel anointed Him king in the place of Saul. Instead, he humbly served the reigning king with his music, then as leader of Saul's army. Although Saul tried to kill his potential rival, David never raised his sword against Saul or against Saul's army. He waited patiently until the Lord dealt with Saul. Even after the evil king's death, David waited another 7½ years before Samuel's prediction was fulfilled.[19] When you seek God's will, explore every option and remain flexible.

10. **Pray and listen.** This last advice encompasses all the rest. While seeking counsel, admitting past error, walking by faith, and remaining alert to various solutions, the Christian will attentively listen to the voice of God.

It is impossible to journey back to the 1500s to understand all the pressures Martin Luther felt. The poverty of his beloved German people, the terror of the Black Plague, the threat of European invasion by Muslim hordes, the accusations of heresy, and the pope's edict of death against him created unbearable stress. He drew comfort from the Psalms and music. He especially loved Psalm 46, on which he based his famous hymn "A Mighty Fortress Is Our God." The psalm concludes, "Be still, and know that I am God; I will be exalted among the nations, I will be exalted in the earth. The LORD Almighty is with us; the God

of Jacob is our fortress" (Psalm 46:10–11). During especially hard days it has been said of Luther,

> He would say to Melanchthon, his faithful coworker,
> "Come, Philip, let us sing the 46th Psalm." And the
> two friends would sing lustily in Luther's own version—
> "Ein feste Burg ist unser Gott." Uncounted wavering,
> doubting, fearful hearts have been strengthened by
> this hymn of faith, have been filled with new courage
> and power to battle for the right to remain true to the
> faith once delivered to the saints.[20]

Our difficulties and struggles pale by comparison to
Luther's, but his solution is still available: *Be still, and know that
I am God; I will be exalted among the nations, I will be exalted in the earth.
The LORD Almighty is with us; the God of Jacob is our fortress.* Pray and
listen, always remembering that the Lord reigns in heaven. He
is not limited in His love, His power, or His knowledge of your
condition. Pray not so much that God would bless your decisions, but rather that you would know His will and have the
courage to pursue it. To know His will is to be well-informed.
To do His will is to be wise. Jesus compared it to building your
home on a solid foundation. He also said, "But everyone who
hears these words of mine and does not put them into practice is like a foolish man who built his house on sand"
(Matthew 7:26). Pray and listen.

How to Know What Is Best, Right, and True

Before you can make a needed change, you must know
what's best. You can learn what's best in a number of
ways, by making mistakes, through instruction, or through the
experience of many years. But mistakes can be painful,
instruction can be misguided, and wisdom doesn't necessari-

ly come with age—sometimes old age shows up alone! David had a better way and disclosed it in the longest of his psalms. He wrote, "Your commands make me wiser than my enemies, for they are ever with me. I have more insight than all my teachers, for I meditate on your statutes. I have more understanding than the elders, for I obey your precepts" (Psalm 119:98–100). Although David was young and inexperienced, he was wiser than his enemies, had more insight than his teachers, and greater understanding than his elders. How? By being a student of God's Word.

You can know what is best, right, and true. The following chapters will discuss how to apply God's truth to bring about constructive and needed change in your life. Life will never be without struggle, but struggle need not be the end of life. Jesus came that we might have an abundant life—a life that includes serenity.

Serenity Principle 3: Know What Is Best, Right, and True

Putting Principle 3 into Action

1. Isolate an issue that needs to be resolved in your life. Do you have a strained friendship? a burdensome credit card debt? a son or daughter struggling in school?
   - First, remember that not every situation is under your control (see Romans 12:18).
   - Focus on what is within your control in the situation: forgiveness, unconditional love, repentance. Think about what you can do to rectify the situation regardless of the other person's faults or blame. Your goal is to resolve the situation, not to point fingers.

- You might seek the advice of a trusted Christian friend or counselor before acting on your decision. This exercise will almost always show how much easier it is to know what is best, right, and true. *Doing* it— that's the hard thing.

2. Did any of the "controversial" statements on page 116 strike you as wrong? Are any close to your heart?

   - Review the Scripture passages listed. Use a Bible Concordance to find other Scripture references on the topic. Study the references.

   - Ask God to help you understand His position on these subjects.

Pray to Know What Is Best, Right, and True

Dear Jesus, You once described Yourself as the way, the truth, and the life. I want to know the way. I want to discover the truth for my situation. And I want to enjoy life again. Help me know the course my life should take. Give me focus, Lord, as I sort out all the confusion and decide on a course of action. Surround me with good counsel and guide me through the indwelling of Your own Holy Spirit. Set my feet back on the secure path of righteousness. Forgive, renew, and restore me, gracious Lord. Thank You for Your Word of truth. Amen.

Principle 4

Honesty Must Precede Change

Consider the true story of Mimi Brodsky Chenfeld's discussion with her 10-year-old friend, Lisa.

Lisa is 10. We are driving together on a Saturday afternoon and talking about the wonderful computer in her classroom.

"It can do everything! It has so much power! It's so much fun!"

She loves that computer.

I am honest about my feelings. I tell her that I believe in the power of good teachers, not in machines. Do computers have laps? Can computers hug? Do computers have shoulders to cry on? When do computers surprise us with spontaneous, unsolicited ideas?

I ask Lisa, "Which would you rather have? An interesting, challenging, exciting teacher or your computer?"

She answers without hesitation, "I'd rather have my computer than my teacher."

I am stunned. "Why?"

"Well, the computer is ..." She searches for words, the right word, "the computer is warm!*"*

"WARM?" I am shouting.

*"Yeah, the computer is warm and my teacher is ..." she narrows her eyes, "*cold.*"*

I am speechless.

"The computer," she continues, "is ... comforting. It's encouraging. If you make a mistake, it says, 'Try again.' or

'Better luck next time.' If you get it right, it says, 'Good job!'
or 'Fine job.' It's comforting."

"What about your teacher?" I ask. I am almost afraid to
ask, but Lisa is pouring out her feelings.

"She never says, 'Good job.' She never tells us we did well.
She's never satisfied. We're never good enough for her. No
matter how great you do, she never tells you she's pleased."

As we drive along, I admit to myself that given the choice
between a machine programmed to be comforting, warm, and
encouraging and a teacher who programs herself to be negative,
discouraging, and cold, I too would choose the machine!

Lisa's confession haunts me. At home, I walk our dogs and
meet almost 3-year-old Tia at the peak of celebrating her first
success at skipping. We cheer for her. "Yaaaaay! Right on!
Super Skipper!" We applaud, smile, hug. Tia skips down the
driveway, eyes shining with pride and accomplishment. I
remember back to Tia's major steps: walking, talking, and now
skipping. Each stage accompanied by affectionate encouragement and praise from family and friends.

When does the celebrating of learning stop?

Lisa's feelings about the warmth of her computer
and the cold of her teacher continue to obsess me. I think
about 7-year-old Andrew, who rushed excitedly into his
house one day after school.

"Mom," he called, "we have a new teacher. The best,
the very best teacher I ever had!"

"But I thought you liked your other teacher," Andrew's
mother wondered.

"I do, but our new teacher is the best. Our other teacher
said, 'No … No … No …' and our new teacher says,
'Yes! Yes! Yes!' "[21]

Wow! If you're a teacher or a parent, that story hits home.

The Bible says, "Better is open rebuke than hidden love. Wounds from a friend can be trusted, but an enemy multiplies kisses" (Proverbs 27:5–6). The fourth serenity principle is *honesty must precede change*. Before a bad situation can be changed, it must be honestly assessed. Before a difficult, unchangeable condition can be accepted, the truth must be known. The first three principles acknowledged the inevitable nature of change, the difficulty of accomplishing change, and the fact that we can know what is best for us. Now we turn our attention to the actual steps we can take toward the serenity God intends for His children. Jesus said, "Peace I leave with you; My peace I give you. I do not give to you as the world gives. Do not let your hearts be troubled and do not be afraid" (John 14:27). The first step toward that peace is a heartfelt admission of need.

This too is God's work. What He expects, He always provides. Our "Declaration of Dependence," as Zig Ziglar likes to describe the day he decided to "let go and let God", is accomplished when the Lord Himself stirs our conscience and troubles us with His Word. He is the faithful Friend who wounds our egos for our own benefit. Paul thanked the Lord for helping him see error he had never recognized before reading God's Word (see Romans 7:7). Like leprosy, sin first appears as only a harmless splotch, nothing to be concerned about. But before it has finished its destructive course, it can rob its victims of all joy in life and any hope of the life to come. How subtle but deadly sin can be. James wrote of its progressive nature, "Each one is tempted when, by his own evil desire, he is dragged away and enticed. Then, after desire has conceived, it gives birth to sin; and sin, when it is full-grown, gives birth to death" (James 1:14–15). The first step toward serenity is an honest appraisal of the present situation.

We Are All Blind to Something

When our youngest son turned 16, Carol and I knew our prayer life was about to attain a new level of intensity. Jacob's older brother, while by no means a saint, is deliberate and careful and tends to play it safe. None of those words describe Jacob, who is fun-loving, risk-taking, spontaneous, and unpredictable. We told Jacob we would continue to pray for his safety, especially as he was taking on the responsibility of driving. We urged him to respect the privilege he now had as a licensed driver.

Did Jacob heed our prayerful concern? Remember the proverb from the last chapter? "When the student is ready, the teacher will appear." Jacob was not ready to listen. He wasn't deliberately disobedient, he was simply oblivious to the potential for danger. Nothing I said, no heartfelt concern expressed by his mother, or loss of privilege seemed to make an impact on Jacob's sense of responsibility behind the wheel. He was invincible. I once came back to my hotel room to find this message on the recorder:

> Hi Dad. Hope everything is going well for you at the conference. Everything is okay here too. I went out to eat with some friends after school and then to the game. We lost, but it was a good game. It's been raining here. I hope it's better where you are. I also got in an accident last night. I couldn't see the road, and it was raining. I know you are disappointed. So am I. I don't know what else to say. Guess I'll see you when you get back home.

It's no wonder insurance rates are so high for teenagers, especially teenage boys. My insurance agent shared a news article that said the likelihood of 16-year-old boys having an accident was more than 100 percent! In other words, enough

16-year-old boys have multiple accidents to offset those who have none. Within the next two years Jacob was in more accidents than his mother or I have experienced in our 25 years of driving. He wasn't always driving, nor at fault, but it seemed hopeless for a time. How could we get through to him? Honesty must precede change. Before Jacob realized the potential dangers of driving, he had to experience the consequence of his mistakes. Unfortunately, that is often the case.

In his book *I'll Quit Tomorrow*, Dr. Vernon Johnson describes the necessity of using crisis creatively to break through the self-deceptive defenses of the chemically dependent. The key to making a change is presenting the truth in such a way that it can be received. Although chemical dependence presents its own special challenge, the same principles apply to anyone whose life is spinning out of control. Johnson advises,

> *Our basic assumption is that even at his sickest, the chemically dependent person can accept reality if it is presented to him in a receivable form ... The rules for conducting this sort of scene can be simply stated.*
>
> 1. *Meaningful persons must present the facts or data.*
> 2. *The data presented should be specific and descriptive of events which have happened or conditions which do exist. Opinions are to be avoided.*
> 3. *The tone of the confrontation should not be judgmental.*
> 4. *The chief evidence should be tied directly into drinking whenever possible.*
> 5. *The evidence of behavior should be presented in some detail.*
> 6. *The goal of the intervention ... is to have him see and accept ... his need for help.*
> 7. *At this point, the available choices acceptable to the interveners may be offered.*[22]

The entire process of intervention is established for one purpose only—to present the honest truth in such a way that the out-of-control person will hit bottom and make the change before he kills himself or someone else. Honesty always precedes change.

Sometimes that honesty comes at a high cost. One rainy night while on his way to an evening worship service, Jacob was hit head-on in an accident that could have easily claimed his life or left him paralyzed. He was not at fault, and no one suffered any major injuries, but we spent some frightful hours next to his bed in prayer. His head and neck were strapped tightly to a spinal board in an emergency medical unit, and he lapsed in and out of consciousness. Fortunately, he was wearing a seat belt and must have been shielded by angels. When I picked up his personal belongings from the demolished compact car, I wondered how anyone could have survived such a massive collision. We are glad to say Jacob has changed his attitude about driving and being invincible. He now drives as safely as anyone can in a large city. A healthy dose of reality always precedes change.

Are You Perfect?

The first step toward accepting correction is to admit that we are not perfect. It is not as easy as it sounds or as sensible as it seems. People always have a hard time admitting their own failings. The Bible leaves no room for those who argue their own perfection. John wrote, "If we claim to be without sin, we deceive ourselves and the truth is not in us. If we confess our sins, He is faithful and just and will forgive us our sins and purify us from all unrighteousness. If we claim we have not sinned, we make Him out to be a liar and His word has no place in our lives" (1 John 1:8–10).

We must not only admit our own failings, we must also accept responsibility for them. Until we do, no real change can take place. But that's not a popular position these days. In California, the Menendez brothers pumped eight rounds of ammunition into their parents and claimed killing them was justified by years of abuse. Damian Williams was clearly shown in a news video bashing the head of truck driver Reginald Denny with a brick during the Los Angeles riots of 1992. His victory dance for the camera showed no signs of remorse. Still he was acquitted of the most serious charges on the grounds he had been deprived as a black child in a white-dominated world. Lorena Bobbit used a knife to disfigure her husband to end his "reign of terror." Never mind that they were legally separated for almost a year and lived a hundred miles apart. She too was acquitted on the grounds of prolonged verbal abuse. How would any of these situations have changed if either party had admitted failure and taken responsibility for it? It sounds like such a simple thing but when you think of the ramifications it could have on criminal behavior in our society, it's staggering.

When Serenity Is Lost, Something's Wrong

When serenity is lost, something's wrong. Notice I didn't say when things go badly, something's wrong. The life of the most faithful Christian is often turbulent and difficult. Knowing Christ is no guarantee of smooth sailing—a quick reading of Hebrews 11 will convince anyone of that fact. The chapter concludes by saying,

> *Some faced jeers and flogging, while still others were chained and put in prison. They were stoned; they were sawed in two; they were put to death by the sword.*

They went about in sheepskins and goatskins, destitute, persecuted and mistreated—the world was not worthy of them. They wandered in deserts and mountains, and in caves and holes in the ground. These were all commended for their faith, yet none of them received what had been promised. God had planned something better for us so that only together with us would they be made perfect.
(Hebrews 11:36–40)

Despite these difficulties, the Bible also says, "You will keep in perfect peace him whose mind is steadfast, because he trusts in You. Trust in the LORD forever, for the LORD, the LORD, is the Rock eternal" (Isaiah 26:3–4). The solution to a lack of serenity is careful examination. A good father never lets a vulnerable child out of his sight. Neither does God. The distance is bridged through confession. James describes it this way, "Come near to God and He will come near to you. Wash your hands, you sinners, and purify your hearts, you double-minded. Grieve, mourn and wail. Change your laughter to mourning and your joy to gloom. Humble yourselves before the Lord, and He will lift you up" (James 4:8–10). Honesty precedes change. Admission of sin is the first step toward the honesty that enables change.

Gaining Objectivity

It is hard to be honest with ourselves. Elaine Viets is a nationally syndicated columnist who has a gift for getting at the heart of serious issues in a humorous way. In one of my favorite columns she tackled the most difficult of all topics, getting people to admit their children might just be average. If there is one area where normally intelligent, well-balanced people lose all objectivity, it is in describing their children. She interviewed a mother of two who actually admitted her children were average:

Lauren Davis seems to be an ordinary woman. But look again. She's a woman of distinction.

"I have the only average children in West County [Suburban St. Louis]," Lauren said. "All the other kids out here are exceptional. Don't get me wrong. I have cute kids. They're not defective or anything. They're just average. That's what makes them so different."

Lauren's family is average-sized. She has two children, Jeremy, 12, and Erin, 7½.

"They're both in the middle reading groups. I let them watch TV. They like B movies. My daughter likes junk food. She thinks Little Debbies are a basic food group." ...

Jeremy and Erin showed signs of averageness early on. They walked and talked when the baby books said they would.

In kindergarten, I asked my son to sound out the word 'cat.' He went through each letter: 'C ... A ... T.'

" 'Pull the sounnds together,' I said encouragingly. 'Africa!' the kid said. I knew then and there that this was not Yale and Harvard."

When challenged by Elaine to admit that not every West County child makes straight A's, Lauren agreed, but added, "Their parents always have a reason why."

Here are some of Lauren's favorites:

- "She's sensitive but doesn't test well."
- "He wasn't feeling well."
- "The air conditioner wasn't working and the room was too warm."
- "The school was too noisy."

And my [Elaine's] personal favorite:

- "The teacher's not challenging her. She's so bored she can't do well."[23]

If we are willing to admit we're not perfect, the second important step to making a change in a positive direction is to gain some objectivity. Ask people you respect what they think about your situation. If money issues are troubling you, seek the advice of a financial planner. Almost every financial institution has people who will help you reorganize your life, consolidate your bills, and plan a budget. If it's workaholism, anxiety, substance abuse, depression, or weight-loss issues, consult someone who has the courage to look you in the eye and tell you the truth. You may have to go back several times. Denial is a part of your problem, or you would have made course-correction years ago.

Find a Safe Place to Come Clean

No amount of self-discovery, recognition of error, or objective analysis will do any good unless we come clean. There is a difference between contrition and repentance. Contrition is the admission of error that leads to sorrow over mistakes made. Many people continue self-destructive behavior while feeling very sorry about it. Repentance implies much more. To repent of failure implies a commitment to turn from error and begin a new free life.

Honesty precedes change. To be honest we must acknowledge our hopeless condition as a first step out of the mire. King David said, "When I kept silent, my bones wasted away through my groaning all day long. For day and night Your hand was heavy upon me; my strength was sapped as in the heat of summer. Then I acknowledged my sin to You and did not cover up my iniquity. I said, 'I will confess my transgressions to the LORD'—and You forgave the guilt of my sin" (Psalm 32:3–5).

We need a safe place to come clean. That safe place may

be with a close friend, a dear spouse, or a respected Christian leader. There is something therapeutic about confession. It is certainly biblical. James made it an important part of his instructions related to healing when he wrote, "Is any one of you sick? He should call the elders of the church to pray over him and anoint him with oil in the name of the Lord. And the prayer offered in faith will make the sick person well; the Lord will raise him up. If he has sinned, he will be forgiven. *Therefore confess your sins to each other and pray for each other so that you may be healed.* The prayer of a righteous man is powerful and effective" (James 5:14–16, emphasis added).

By admitting our sins, we acknowledge that there is nothing barring our access to God's throne of grace. Or, as Paul put it, "He [Jesus] took it [our sin] away, nailing it to the cross" (Colossians 2:14). The sin that held us captive is released by the power of the cross and the command of Christ. He told His disciples, "If you forgive anyone his sins, they are forgiven; if you do not forgive them, they are not forgiven" (John 20:23). That same authority was given to all Christians when Jesus said, "tell it to the church. ... whatever you loose [forgive] on earth will be loosed in heaven" (Matthew 18:17–18). Confession is good for the soul. As rain cleans the air and leaves it refreshed, an honest assessment of our present situation can cleanse the soul and bring hope.

It Isn't the End, but It's a Good Beginning

Accepting the truth about ourselves and our need for help is not the end, but it's a good beginning. In later chapters we will learn how God's Word, prayer, Christian friends, and the establishment of different life patterns can help us achieve needed change in our lives. Every journey begins with one step. The first step toward serenity is honesty.

Serenity Principle 4:
Honesty Must Precede Change

Putting Principle 4 into Action

1. Make a list of those people who've hurt you deeply in the past. Include the things they did that brought you pain.

   - Read Psalm 130 and Romans 12:17–21. Jesus said, "If you forgive men when they sin against you, your heavenly Father will also forgive you. But if you do not forgive men their sins, your Father will not forgive your sins" (Matthew 6:14–15). Knowing how important it is for you to forgive the sins of others before you can receive the forgiveness you need, offer a prayer of forgiveness on their behalf, naming each one on your list.

   - Destroy your list as a symbol of the complete forgiveness you receive through Jesus.

2. Identify an area of your life that needs change. Ask a Christian you trust for suggestions about making change.

   - Tell him you want to change that part of your life and (as we read in James 5) ask for his prayers on your behalf.

   - Ask him to check with you in a month to see how it's going.

3. Review the list of suggestions from Dr. Vernon Johnson's book *I'll Quit Tomorrow* (page 131).

   - Why do you think his procedure has been so successful in helping family and friends conduct interventions with chemically dependent people?

   - How can those suggestions be applied to the changes you need to make in your life?

Pray for Honesty

Lord, it is so easy to be honest about others and so difficult to be honest about myself. Help me to make an honest assessment of my present situation and to find a safe place to come clean. I know I need to do more than admit my sin. Like King David, I know my condition is hopeless, but I also know that when I confess my sin to You, You will forgive me. There is nothing keeping me from Your throne of grace, Lord. For that I thank You. In Jesus' name. Amen.

Principle 5

God Can Change People

Accomplishing change in people is the single greatest challenge of those in positions of leadership. Five-star General H. Norman Schwarzkopf, in a speech the subject of leadership, said, "Leadership is not the same as competency. There are many competent people in the world who can get a job done, but it is not always achieved through the exercise of leadership. Leadership is the ability to get people to do willingly what they ordinarily would not do."[24] Easier said than done!

If a situation is unmovable, then as the famous prayer conveys, we must "accept the things I cannot change." The ability to change is crucial to the achievement of serenity. People who can't accept what they cannot change will be forever miserable. When the Lord confronted Paul on the road to Damascus, Paul was zealously fighting against God. The Lord asked Paul, "Saul, Saul, why do you persecute Me? It is hard for you to kick against the goads" (Acts 26:14). A goad was a prodding stick used by Israelite farmers to urge their oxen on as they plowed. It was often pointed and sometimes tipped with iron. If a team of oxen faithfully performed their duty, no prodding was necessary. If they refused, the jab of the goad was soon to follow. The phrase *kicking against the goad* described a person who brought needless pain upon himself by stubborn disobedience or refusal to accept the inevitable. Those who kick against the goads of life will never know the peace that surpasses understanding.

God can change people. It is the fifth biblical principle of change. Saul changed. He had been a Jew's Jew, perfect according to their standards: "Circumcised on the eighth day, of the people of Israel, of the tribe of Benjamin, a Hebrew of Hebrews; in regard to the law, a Pharisee; as for zeal, persecuting the church; as for legalistic righteousness, faultless" (Philippians 3:5–6). But God took a Jewish Pharisee named Saul and made him Paul, a missionary to the Gentiles. Even his name was changed. His Hebrew name—Shaul—was probably chosen by his parents at the time of his birth. It means "desired one" or "asked for." The name Paul is a Greek name he took for himself after his conversion. Paul means "small" or "insignificant." What a change! From a proud man to a humble servant. Before his conversion he described himself as "advancing in Judaism beyond many Jews of my own age ... extremely zealous for the traditions of my fathers" (Galatians 1:14). After his conversion he described himself as "chief of sinners" (see 1 Timothy 1:15 KJV).

Paul realized there was nothing to be gained by opposing God. It was a sure path to frustration and certain defeat. Enough goad-kicking for Paul. When Ananias was asked by God to talk to Paul about his new purpose, he was afraid to go. Saul had a reputation for imprisoning and killing Christians. God told Ananias things had changed: "He is praying" (Acts 9:11). Saul was done with his old life and was praying to know his new purpose. If you are done with your old life, be assured God can and does change people. He changed Saul into Paul. He can change you too.

A Miraculous Story of Personal Change

When Corrie ten Boom was in her late teens, she attended a Christian conference where she met Christian missionaries from around the world. She returned home filled with excitement and optimism. Her father, listening to her enthusiastic retelling of the experience commented, "Isn't it wonderful to have such joy here on earth? It's a little foretaste of heaven. Yet, the best is yet to be." Corrie remembered that expression as one her father frequently used to remind his children of their ultimate destination. But things would get worse before they got better. Corrie and her entire family were ravaged by Hitler's reign of terror. She watched as her beloved sister, Betsie, slipped from this world to the next, destroyed by the horrors of life in a Nazi concentration camp. How could a bright-eyed, innocent and kind young woman from Holland suffer the cruel brutality of a concentration camp without breaking into a million pieces of shattered humanity? The Lord enabled her to accept what she could not change. Her biographers were amazed at her story. But more than her story, they were amazed at her face, which radiated love, peace, and joy, despite her ordeal. From her they learned not only of Nazi atrocities but also, more important, lessons of life, which they enumerated:

- Handling separation
- Getting along with less
- Security in the midst of insecurity
- Forgiveness
- How God can use weakness
- Facing death
- Dealing with difficult people
- How to love your enemies
- What to do when evil wins[25]

To what degree was Corrie able to accept what she could not change? That question is best demonstrated by the incident of the fleas. As the war's tide turned, Germany moved prisoners to camps within their own country. Corrie and Betsie were moved to Ravensbrück. Conditions were filthy and over-crowded. A building designed to hold 400 women was crammed with 1,400. Platforms made to sleep four were crowded to the point of breaking. Eight toilets, overflowing with filth, were horribly inadequate. The platforms were covered with straw, and the straw was filled with fleas.

Despite such desperate conditions, Betsie gave thanks to God that she was able to keep her Bible by hiding it beneath her clothes. The first passage Corrie and Betsie read upon their arrival in Ravensbrück was from Paul's letter to the church at Thessalonica.

> *Encourage the timid, help the weak, be patient with every-*
> *one. Make sure that nobody pays back wrong for wrong,*
> *but always try to be kind to each other and to everyone else.*
> *Be joyful always; pray continually; give thanks in all*
> *circumstances, for this is God's will for you in Christ Jesus.*
> (1 *Thessalonians* 5:14–18)

Betsie decided that the sisters needed to focus on their blessings not their troubles. Corrie was urged to pray a prayer of thanks. At first it was difficult to think of anything to be thankful about, but Betsie persisted: "for being together ... for the Bible they had been able to keep ... for the overcrowding." Corrie balked at thanking God for overcrowding until Betsie reminded her that with people packed so closely, more would hear their devotions. She even asked Corrie to pray a prayer of thanks for the fleas!

Corrie complained. "This was too much. 'Betsie, there's no way even God can make me grateful for a flea.' 'Give thanks in *all* circumstances,' [Betsie] quoted. 'It doesn't say, "in pleas-ant circumstances." Fleas are part of this place where God has put us.' And so we stood between piers of bunks and gave thanks for fleas. But this time I was sure Betsie was wrong."[26]

As it turned out, Betsie was right. The crowded conditions allowed more people to hear the sisters' daily Scripture lesson. The lesson was translated from one language to another across the room from Dutch to German, to French, to Polish, to Russian, to Czech. It seemed like a preview of heaven where every tongue from every nation will be gathered to give praise to the Lord. So many prisoners wanted to hear the nightly readings and prayers that the ten Booms were forced to add a second evening service after roll call. The degree of freedom they enjoyed in the confines of their barracks continued to amaze them. They lived virtually undisturbed in their crammed quarters. It was only later, when a guard was called but refused to enter, that they discovered the reason for their freedom— the fleas! The place was infested with fleas to such a degree that the guards wouldn't come. Corrie learned that God provided blessing even through adversity. When circumstances can't be changed, pray that God will change you.

The greatest change of all came after the war. Betsie died in Ravensbrück. Corrie was released only by virtue of a clerical error. Almost immediately, Corrie began to make good on her promise to tell others all that she and Betsie had learned. Once, after sharing her testimony of God's goodness at a church service in Munich, Corrie was confronted by a former SS guard who had mocked the women at the showers in the camp at Ravensbrück. Corrie recounts her feelings:

> His hand was thrust out to shake mine. And I, who had preached so often to the people in Bloemendaal the need to forgive, kept my hand at my side.
>
> Even as the angry, vengeful thoughts boiled through me, I saw the sin of them. Jesus Christ had died for this

man; was I going to ask for more? Lord Jesus, I prayed, forgive me and help me to forgive him.

I tried to smile, I struggled to raise my hand. I could not. I felt nothing, not the slightest spark of warmth or charity. And so again I breathed a silent prayer. Jesus, I cannot forgive him. Give me Your forgiveness.

As I took his hand the most incredible thing happened. From my shoulder along my arm and through my hand a current seemed to pass from me to him, while into my heart sprang a love for this stranger that almost over-whelmed me.

And so I discovered that it is not on our forgiveness any more than on our goodness that the world's healing hinges, but on His. When He tells us to love our enemies, He gives, along with the command, the love itself.[27]

God can change people. He changed Paul. He changed Corrie ten Boom and a Nazi prison guard. He can change you.

Feelings Follow Actions

Like Corrie ten Boom we want to do what is right but don't feel capable. We say to ourselves, "When I get over my hurt, then I'll forgive. When I feel generous, then I'll give. When I quit hurting, then I'll go out and face the world again." It doesn't work that way. If Corrie had waited on her feelings, the former Nazi guard would have gone unforgiven, and her bitterness and anger would have continued to imprison Corrie. She did the right thing. Feelings follow actions.

Jesus said, "Where your treasure is, there your heart will be also" (Matthew 6:21). Many Christians like to turn that passage on its head by saying, "Where your heart is, your treasure will follow," but that's not the way Jesus said it. If you want to accomplish a difficult change, invest yourself. Give your time, effort, and financial support to those things you value or want to value. Don't wait for a good feeling to motivate you. It's a simple three-step process:

1. Identify the issue.
2. Seek God's will on it.
3. Begin acting as God directs.

If His will is contrary to your own, it will require change for you—change that will go against your natural inclinations. There is no easy way to partially trust the wisdom of God. You either do or you don't. The prophet said, " 'Bring the whole tithe into the storehouse, that there may be food in my house. *Test Me in this*,' says the LORD Almighty, 'and see if I will not throw open the floodgates of heaven and pour out so much blessing that you will not have room enough for it' " (Malachi 3:10, emphasis added). In this or any other issue, we are asked to check our feelings and trust His promises. We are simply directed to do the right thing.

A spouse who waits for her "feelings" to return before making an effort to renew or restore a marriage is walking a dangerous path. But the spouse who knows and trusts Scripture will not wait for things to get better before taking action. She will take the initiative and *make* things better out of obedience to the Lord who said, "Do nothing out of selfish ambition or vain conceit, but in humility consider others better than yourselves. Each of you should look not only to your own interests, but also to the interests of others" (Philippians 2:3–4). Faithful Christians know God can change people.

Don't misunderstand—feelings are important. God wants our actions to come from a willing heart. But when it's hard to love and hard to obey God's directives, Christians look to the love of Christ for their motivation. As Paul said,

"Bear with each other and forgive whatever grievances you may have against one another. *Forgive as the Lord forgave you.* ... And whatever you do, whether in word or deed, *do it all in the name of the Lord Jesus,* giving thanks to God the Father through Him" (Colossians 3:13, 17, emphasis added). Let His love be your motive until your obedience can bring about a change of heart.

Life is better because of feelings. What would we be without love, heartache, desire, passion, fear, and anticipation? Cherish your feelings. Even the sadness of a loved one's death is an indication of the blessing of life. Feelings are from God. The Psalms of David are packed with feelings of every kind and are loved because of it. Feelings are good, but they are not the best way to determine right from wrong. God's Word is given as our only reliable guide to truth. When His truth validates our feelings, it's a wonderful thing. When Scripture stands in opposition to our feelings, His Word—not our feelings—must dominate.

God Is Right Even When He Seems Wrong

As a pastor, I've taken unpopular positions more than once. An unmarried couple living together can suggest many logical reasons for their decision. "We've both experienced a divorce in the past, and we're just afraid it could happen again." Or "When we are both working, living together makes it possible for someone to be with the kids and keep their schedule." Or "It allows time for the children to get to know the potential husband or wife." Or "It helps pay the bills." Or "It eliminates the pretension that a dating relationship can perpetuate." Or "It saves money by eliminating the expense of dating." All the "reasons" people give for compromising God's Word could fill a book. But God is right even when He seems wrong. His Word is clear: "Marriage should be honored by all, and the marriage bed kept pure, for God will judge the adulterer and all the sexually immoral" (Hebrews 13:4). The Sixth Commandment still applies: "You shall not commit adultery" (Exodus 20:14). It's hard to hear that something you're doing is wrong. But if you want to change, you need God's help.

A house built to last needs a good foundation. A life built to last must have the same quality. Jesus said,

> Everyone who hears these words of Mine and puts them into practice is like a wise man who built his house on the rock. The rain came down, the streams rose, and the winds blew and beat against that house; yet it did not fall, because it had its foundation on the rock. But everyone who hears these words of Mine and does not put them into practice is like a foolish man who built his house on sand. The rain came down, the streams rose, and the winds blew and beat against that house, and it fell with a great crash.
> (Matthew 7:24–27)

God's formula for standing against temptation is simple but profound. He says, "Submit yourselves, then, to God. Resist the devil, and he will flee from you" (James 4:7). Notice that submission to God precedes any attempt to resist the devil. If you get that backwards you'll never withstand the storm when it breaks against your house.

The Best Is Yet to Come

When Corrie ten Boom told her family of the great joy she had experienced at a Christian retreat, her father reminded her, "The best is yet to come." Years later, when his entire family was arrested for helping Jews escape the Nazi persecution in Holland, he repeated those words to Corrie. The Gestapo officer was kind at first. He told the old man he could go home if he would give his word not to hide Jews or cause the German army any more trouble. Corrie said she could not see his face but will never forget the dignity of his stance and the clarity of his answer. "'If I go home today,' he said evenly and clearly, 'tomorrow I will open my door again to any man in need who knocks.'"[28] As they ushered him off to certain death, he told his daughter, "Remember, Corrie, the best is yet to be."[29]

Two truths are sure:

1. Difficult times never last.
2. Nothing earth offers is worth comparing
   to the glories of heaven.

When Moses lived in Pharaoh's house, he lacked nothing the world could offer. He drank from golden goblets, wore the finest linen, and received an education second to none. He gave it all up for something better:

> He chose to be mistreated along with the people of God rather than to enjoy the pleasures of sin for a short time. He regarded disgrace for the sake of Christ as of greater value than the treasures of Egypt, because he was looking ahead to his reward. By faith he left Egypt, not fearing the king's anger; he persevered because he saw Him who is invisible.
>
> (Hebrews 11:25–27)

The decision Moses made was a difficult one, but wise. He knew that God's blessing was more important (and better) than all the riches of Egypt. The same motive enabled Jesus to endure the cross. The Bible tells us, "Let us fix our eyes on Jesus, the author and perfecter of our faith, *who for the joy set before* Him endured the cross, scorning its shame, and sat down at the right hand of the throne of God" (Hebrews 12:2, emphasis added). The best was yet to come for Jesus as He entered His glory. Knowing the outcome in advance helped Him find strength to endure the momentary suffering of the cross. The same truth can help us find serenity in difficulty.

The Bible says, "Let us not become weary in doing good, for at the proper time we will reap a harvest if we do not give up" (Galatians 6:9). *The best is yet to come.* The growing season can be long and difficult. It's no fun to plow the hard soil, rake the clods, and prepare the ground for planting. And I never enjoyed pulling weeds and watering the parched plants under the hot July sun. But when the tomatoes ripened and the sweet corn was ready for picking, then the work seemed worthwhile. Knowing the outcome can help you sustain your resolve when times are difficult. I've often quoted Paul's words to Christians in deep water. He said, "I consider that our present sufferings are not worth comparing with the glory that will be revealed in us" (Romans 8:18). Paul knew the same secret that Corrie ten Boom's father knew: *The best is yet to come.*

The fifth serenity principle is *God can change people.* He can, He has, and He does. What needs changing in your life? Remember these simple truths:

1. Feelings follow actions.
2. God is right even when He seems wrong.
3. The best is yet to come.

These simple truths may be just the help you need to make the change you've been praying for.

Serenity Principle 5:
God Can Change People

Putting Principle 5 into Action

1. Identify a characteristic or attitude in yourself that you would like to change.

   - Acknowledge that you need God's help to change that attitude or characteristic.

   - Look up the following Bible stories about change:

     o David's change from adulterous king to forgiven king (2 Samuel 11:1–12:25)

     o Jonah's change from a runaway to a servant of God (Jonah 1:1–3:10)

     o Hannah's change from bitterness to dependence on God (1 Samuel 1:1–2:11)

   - How did God work change in each of these lives? How did David, Jonah, and Hannah learn to depend on God?

   - How do the lessons of David, Jonah, and Hannah apply to the change *you* want to accomplish?

2. What teaching of the Bible do you find most difficult to accept?

   - How do your "feelings" on this subject make it more difficult to accept God's position?

   - A teenager once said, "I used to be against abortion, but then I got pregnant." How can personal situations make it difficult to maintain objectivity?

   - Pray about the teaching you listed at the beginning of this question. Ask God to help you understand His plans for you.

Pray for God's Help in Making a Personal Change

G racious Lord, the Bible says You know all things so You already know I find some things in Your Word difficult to accept. I want to do the right thing. Forgive my arrogance and pride. Like Corrie, I'm not inclined to give You thanks for fleas and difficulties in life. Open my eyes to see how Your way is really best for my life. When I walk toward the light, encourage me with Your blessing. When I walk toward the darkness, frustrate my path and restore me to faithfulness. I believe You can change people. Change me, Lord, to be more like You. Change the people I love, Lord, who seem committed to a life contrary to Your will. I ask all these things in Jesus' name. Amen.

Principle 6
God Can Change Situations

Gentlemen,

I came across this prayer a while back when down at the Boy Scout office. Although I'm not a big MacArthur fan (his post-WWII arrogance was largely responsible for great loss in Korea[30]) this prayer grows on me the more I read it, and it is always nice to learn about a praying hero. Wouldn't it be great if we could actually speak with the author to learn his state of mind when he wrote this, or to ask what he meant by certain statements ...?

No matter, I thought you might enjoy the read.

Mark

Mark has been a friend for many years. We've attended Promise Keepers rallies together with our sons. He's also one of the men who holds me accountable as a father, husband, and Christian brother. Mark loves to read and often shares his findings with his Christian friends. Here's the famous prayer Mark included with his note:

Build me a son, O Lord, who will be strong enough to know when he is weak, and brave enough to face himself when he is afraid; one who will be proud and unbending in honest defeat, humble and gentle in victory.

Build me a son whose wishes will not take the place of deeds; a son who will know Thee—and that to know himself is the foundation stone of knowledge.

Lead him, I pray, not in the path of ease and comfort, but under the stress and spur of difficulties and challenge.

Here let him learn to stand up in the storm; here let him learn compassion for those who fail.

Build me a son whose heart will be clear, whose goal will be high; a son who will master himself before he seeks to master other men; one who will reach into the future, yet never forget the past.

And after all these things are his, add, I pray, enough of a sense of humor, so that he may always be serious, yet never take himself too seriously. Give him humility, so that he may always remember the simplicity of true greatness, the open mind of true wisdom, and the meekness of true strength.

Then, I, his father, will dare to whisper, 'I have not lived in vain.'

General Douglas MacArthur[31]

General MacArthur's prayer came to mind when I was asked to write a letter to a young man in my congregation who was about to celebrate his 16th birthday. His folks are humble, hardworking people, devoted to the cause of Christ and their family. They were following the advice of Robert Lewis' excellent book, *Raising a Modern-Day Knight*. Lewis proposes that Christian parents follow an intentional course of training their sons to be godly men. The celebration of a son's 16th birthday, considered a rite of passage in American culture, is suggested as a perfect time to conduct a ceremony of commitment. According to Lewis, the commitment should include a pledge to keep 10 biblical principles that he calls the "chain links in the Code of Conduct" for a godly man. They include loyalty, servant-leadership, kindness, humility, purity, honesty, self-discipline, excellence, integrity, and perseverance.

These parents were concerned about their son's ability to transcend his humble origins and achieve his life's goal of entering full-time Christian ministry as a teacher. Paul, they said, was troubled by the academic and financial barriers he would have to overcome to realize his dream. Knowing my background, Paul's parents asked if I would participate in the evening by writing a personal letter to Paul about his concerns. They wanted Paul to know that God can and does change situations. They felt Paul's dreams were stilted by his own limited experience. They knew God could do anything and wanted their son to believe the same. To Paul I wrote:

Dear Paul,

It is my privilege to write you this note on this very special occasion in your life. Your circumstance and mine are a lot more alike than you might think. I grew up in a very modest home. My mother did not work outside the home except for a brief time now and then to catch up past-due bills. My dad was a factory worker. Not many of my relatives (to the best of my knowledge)— my uncles, aunts, grandparents—ever obtained a college education. There is nothing wrong nor detrimental about growing up in a blue-collar family. There is no dishonor, no shame in the way your folks or mine made their living.

You are attending a Christian high school with many people who have grown up differently than you. I grew up in a small Indiana farm town but attended an affluent Christian high school in a larger city, 30 miles from home. A Christian businessman paid for my tuition and the school arranged for my housing. I went home every weekend to see my family and to work at a dairy store. Most people considered me poor.

My schoolmates didn't know much about my life, and I knew little about theirs. The things they talked

about, the cars they drove, the homes they lived in—
everything about their personal life was different than
mine. It was very natural for me to feel inferior. They
had better things so they must be better, *is what* I
thought. Even when I began to be accepted in their
world, I was very careful not to invite them into mine.
I stayed at their homes but they never stayed at mine.
I *thought,* What they don't know won't hurt them.
Many of them just assumed my background was like
theirs—it was my secret. I even stayed in the ROTC
program longer than the mandatory first year because
of the uniforms they issued. I didn't have to worry about
having nice clothes except on Fridays when everyone
dressed in "civilian" attire.

So when did things change for me? When did
I come to realize that I deserved a future as promising
as theirs? Where did I get the confidence to think that
I could write a book that other people would read?
What ever possessed me to believe I would one day teach
leadership skills to other professionals? It started in high
school when I was your age. I worked hard at making
good grades. That was a "level playing field" for me.
I could study harder, spend more time, and go the extra
mile to prove (mostly to myself) that I could compete.
The truth is, I probably wasn't as smart as many of
my friends. It took me twice as much effort to get an A
as it took them, but I had the heart for it, the desire.

Soon it was time to go to college. My folks couldn't
afford a dime for my education and I never expected
them to. The only money they could spare was $80 for
a round-trip bus ticket home at Christmas. The other
holidays I spent with friends who lived near the Christian
college I was attending in Texas. It was enough. I worked

*hard during the summer and saved my money for tuition.
I also worked 20 hours every week during school and used
that money for tuition too. If I wanted spending money,
I took a weekend job raking leaves, or did odd jobs ...
for a while I even donated blood plasma each week for
$5 at a local clinic! I also received financial help because
of my parents' limited income. (I found out being poor
could also have its advantages.) Friends of our family
also helped and occasionally surprised me with a
personal check.*

*Paul, if you want anything enough, you can have
it. The hard road isn't the wrong road. The character
and internal strength I developed through struggle has
served me well over the years. I learned to believe in the
Lord's ability to provide, and in my God-given ability
to succeed. As the apostle Paul said,*

I know what it is to be in need, and I know what
it is to have plenty. I have learned the secret of
being content in any and every situation, whether
well fed or hungry, whether living in plenty or in
want. I can do everything through Him who gives
me strength. (*Philippians* 4:12–13)

*As I look back on those hard times, I realize they
were a blessing, not a curse. I learned more by the
process than I learned from the books. My hero, Booker
T. Washington, was born a slave and yet rose to become
one of America's greatest educators and leaders. Looking
back on his own difficulty he wrote, "Out of the unusual
struggle through which he [the black child] is compelled
to pass, he gets a strength, a confidence, that one misses
whose pathway is comparatively smooth by reason of
birth and race."*[32]

Your struggle, Paul, is not a reason to limit yourself.
Properly understood, it will be an advantage as you
pursue your dreams. What is it you want to do more
than anything else? Your God is able to show His
strength through your weakness. I have never known
a truly great person who couldn't honestly admit that
without God's blessing he was nothing. I have never
forgotten my past. I'm not ashamed of my family roots.
I never allow the limitations of my environment to limit
my dreams. Neither should you.

God especially enjoys achieving great things
through people who know that without Him (and a
lot of help) they could never make it. You are perfectly
positioned to do great things!

Go make a difference in things that matter.
Go make an eternal difference.

Sincerely Yours, Completely His,
Pastor Hower

God Can Change Situations

God delights in changing situations. The Bible is a history of God changing situations. He took a shepherd boy and made him a king. He took an old couple named Abraham and Sarah and made them parents. He took Egyptians' slaves and forged them into a great nation. He used a Pharisee named Paul, an accomplice to murder and a hater of Christians, to preach Jesus to the Gentiles.

When we pray the Serenity Prayer, we ask God for "the courage to change the things I can." We are really asking Him for discernment. We want Him to help us identify those situations that can and should be different. We are also asking for the courage to tackle those situations no matter how impossible they may seem.

Consider the plight of Mary, the mother of Jesus. She was happily going about her life, engaged to be married and making all the usual plans young girls make for their future. But a visit by the angel Gabriel changed everything. Her life was turned upside down. What God asked of Mary was impossible. She was going to give birth but remain a virgin. How could that be?

Although her family lived in obscurity, far from Jerusalem, the angel said her son would "[sit on] the throne of His father David, and reign ... over the house of Jacob forever" (Luke 1:32–33). Mary and Joseph lived more than 100 miles from Bethlehem in the rugged hills of Galilee, but the prophets said their son would be born in Bethlehem of Judea. When Mary told her fiancé, Joseph, all these things, he doubted the truth and decided to divorce her quietly. She must have wondered how she would overcome her situational nightmare. The answer was simple but not easy. Gabriel said, "Nothing is impossible with God" (Luke 1:37).

Although selected for a very special role in God's redemptive work, nothing was made easy for Mary and Joseph. They were required to make a very long journey in the midst of a late-term pregnancy, and they apparently did it without the help and support of family. There is no mention of assistance being given on the road or in Bethlehem. Were they keeping Mary's pregnancy a secret? (The robes of the day could have easily concealed her condition.) It would have been hard to explain Mary's early delivery to family and friends. It took a miracle to convince Joseph!

Did Mary go to Bethlehem with her husband in order to conceal the birth? A typical census did not require the participation of wives and children. Why did the young couple make no attempt to return to Nazareth after Jesus' birth? Were they protecting Mary's reputation? They were still in Bethlehem when it came time for Mary's purification 40 days later. And although the timing of the Magi's visit is subject to debate, many believe their visit (also in Bethlehem) probably occurred more than a year after Jesus' birth. We are told Joseph's young family was no longer living in a stable or even an inn. The Bible says he had secured more permanent lodging in a house when the Eastern visitors arrived.

So many unanswered questions surround the story of Jesus' birth. If it had happened to me and my fiancée, some record of my frustration would have been recorded in Luke's narrative! Why didn't God choose a couple who actually lived in Bethlehem? Why didn't God arrange better conditions for the birth of His own Son? Why should Joseph, Mary, and Jesus flee to Egypt? Why didn't God just strike Herod dead and save everyone a lot of trouble? But no mention is made of Joseph's frustration or any questions he and Mary asked of God for that matter. Once they knew God's will, they trusted Him to handle the details of a virgin pregnancy, a long and difficult journey, poor lodging, and all the rest. They knew God was capable of accomplishing anything He asked them to do. It gives me some comfort to read, "But Mary treasured up all these things and pondered them in her heart" (Luke 2:19). She had a lot to ponder! She saw firsthand that God can accomplish extraordinary things through ordinary people.

The Courage to Change the Things We Can

How do we decide which situations can be changed and which cannot? How does faith enter the picture? If God can do impossible things, is there any situation we should accept as unchangeable?

While all things are possible for God, He does speak about things that are beyond our ability. The matter of salvation is just one example. The Bible says, "No man can redeem the life of another or give to God a ransom for him—the ransom for a life is costly, no payment is ever enough—that he should live on forever and not see decay" (Psalm 49:7–9).

When it comes to living in peace with other people, the Bible also reminds us of natural limitations. Paul wrote, "Do not repay anyone evil for evil. Be careful to do what is right in the eyes of everybody. If it is possible, as far as it depends on you, live at peace with everyone" (Romans 12:17–18). God made people with something called free will. No matter how hard we try, we may not be able to make some people love us. If they can choose to reject God, they can certainly choose to reject us too. That's why God added that important phrase *as far as it depends on you*. He reminds us that a relationship requires the cooperation of two people. No matter how willing you are to make a relationship work, the other person can foil your plans. God's lesson is clear: Let there be nothing in your behavior or your attitude that contributes to the problem. At the same time, accept the fact that some things are outside of your control.

God wants to keep us from frustration over situations that do not change, or may change in a way beyond our ability to control. While nothing is impossible for God, many things are impossible for us. Knowing what we can and cannot do is important to our peace of mind.

The principle of limitation that applies to relationships can also be applied to other situations. When sizing up any challenge, Christians should realize the difference between God's ability and their own. The phrase *as far as it depends on you* applies. A different phrase is used in another passage to teach the same truth. About making plans James wrote, "You ought

to say, 'If it is the Lord's will, we will live and do this or that' "
(James 4:15). It is okay to dream impossible dreams. God even
encourages us to expect His help when undertaking "impossible" situations, especially on behalf of others (see James
4:2–3). But the Lord wants us to know the difference between
the power of positive thinking and divine blessing. The first
has definite limits, and the latter is dependent completely on
the decision of God. No amount of positive thinking, group
dynamics, or self-denial can force God to act against His will.

Questions to Ask before Attempting Change

1. **What is the real motive for attempting this change?** God
   cares a great deal about motives. David charged his son,
   "And you, my son Solomon, acknowledge the God of your
   father, and serve Him with wholehearted devotion and
   with a willing mind, for the LORD searches every heart and
   understands *every motive* behind the thoughts. If you seek
   Him, He will be found by you; but if you forsake Him, He
   will reject you forever" (1 Chronicles 28:9, emphasis
   added). Hanani the seer told Asa, King of Judah, "For the
   eyes of the LORD range throughout the earth to strengthen
   those *whose hearts are fully committed* to Him" (2 Chronicles
   16:9, emphasis added). God looks at the heart. He knows
   your motive. Your heart has to be right and your purpose
   proper to expect God's blessing.

2. **Have you prayed and sought God's counsel in the matter?** Before Paul began his first missionary journey, the
   Bible says, "While they were worshiping the Lord and fasting, the Holy Spirit said, 'Set apart for Me Barnabas and
   Saul for the work to which I have called them.' So *after they
   had fasted and prayed*, they placed their hands on them and
   sent them off" (Acts 13:2–3, emphasis added).

3. **Does this goal require you in any way to violate any aspect of God's Word?** As mentioned earlier, the end never justifies the means in God's sight. "When tempted, no one should say, 'God is tempting me.' For God cannot be tempted by evil, nor does He tempt anyone" (James 1:13).

4. **Does any aspect of this change depend on the action of someone else?** You cannot predict or direct the actions of another. The wicked cannot even control themselves. "The way of the wicked is like deep darkness; they do not know what makes them stumble" (Proverbs 4:19).

5. **Will the accomplishment of this goal bring honor and glory to the Lord?** How will the achievement of this change affect other people? Christians are God's "salt" and "light" in a world of darkness. "Whatever you do, do it all for the glory of God" (1 Corinthians 10:31).

6. **Are you prepared to work hard to accomplish the goal?** Godly goals won't necessarily be easy goals. The devil, the world, and our own sinful flesh wage war against God's desired outcomes. "Whatever your hand finds to do, do it with all your might, for in the grave, where you are going, there is neither working nor planning nor knowledge nor wisdom" (Ecclesiastes 9:10).

7. **Can you be patient and content while working toward the goal?** The difference between working hard to improve yourself and the sin of coveting is a matter of attitude. Success is never contingent on what you own or achieve. "But godliness with contentment is great gain. For we brought nothing into the world, and we can take nothing out of it. But if we have food and clothing, we will be content with that. People who want to get rich fall into temptation and a trap and into many foolish and harmful desires that plunge men into ruin and destruction" (1 Timothy 6:6–9).

8. **Is this a commitment you can keep?** Godly people in the Bible were encouraged to make vows and often did. David said, "Make vows to the LORD your God and fulfill them; let all the neighboring lands bring gifts to the One to be feared" (Psalm 76:11). On the other hand, the Lord urges us to refrain from making commitments we have no intention of fulfilling. "When you make a vow to God, do not delay in fulfilling it. He has no pleasure in fools; fulfill your vow. It is better not to vow than to make a vow and not fulfill it" (Ecclesiastes 5:4–5).

9. **Are respected Christian people supportive of your intention?** Don't overlook the help and advice of trusted Christian friends. "Plans fail for lack of counsel, but with many advisers they succeed" (Proverbs 15:22). Solomon was wise but still advised, "Make plans by seeking advice; if you wage war, obtain guidance" (Proverbs 20:18).

10. **Are your plans open to redirection by the Lord?** Perseverance is not the same as stubbornness. Do you know the difference? It is good to make plans, but it is better to know God's plans. "Listen to advice and accept instruction, and in the end you will be wise. Many are the plans in a man's heart, but it is the LORD's purpose that prevails" (Proverbs 19:20–21).

A Proven Formula to Accomplish Change

God can and does change situations. But how should we seek to involve Him in our plans? How can we best know His intention for our life?

"Ask, seek, and knock" (see Matthew 7:7) is the simple formula Jesus offered on the subject of securing divine help. He based His counsel on the principle of lesser to greater. He said, "Which of you, if his son asks for bread, will give him a stone? Or if he asks for a fish, will give him a snake? If you, then, though you are evil, know how to give good gifts to your children, how much more will your Father in heaven give good gifts to those who ask Him!" (Matthew 7:9–11). If we (who know far less than God) do good things for our children, won't God (who is much wiser than we will ever be) make sure good things are accomplished for Christians?

Ask

It all starts with asking. We ask our heavenly Father for the thing we need or want. We can ask with even greater confidence than a child might ask her loving father for the thing she needs. Of course, asking doesn't guarantee that a father will grant his child's request. Children often ask for foolish and hurtful things, but a father wants to know his child's perceived needs. He wants his child to count on him. Sometimes a father may allow a child he loves to experience difficult and potentially harmful conditions. Even General MacArthur prayed, "Lead him, I pray, not in the path of ease and comfort, but under the stress and spur of difficulties and challenge. Here let him learn to stand up in the storm; here let him learn compassion for those who fail."

We trust God to know what is best. Like Jesus in the Garden of Gethsemane, we must learn the wisdom of praying "may Your will be done" (Matthew 26:42). Our duty is to ask, knowing that God who is wise and good will respond according to His love for our good.

Seek

We are to seek. Our challenges never exist in a vacuum. Seek God's counsel in His Word. Seek the counsel of other Christian friends. Seek solutions by the natural and practical means that God has placed at your disposal. God expects us to act. He tells us to "walk by faith, not by sight" (2 Corinthians 5:7 KJV). The Greek word for *walk* literally means "make progress down a path." We are to move along the narrow road not knowing exactly where it leads. As though in a fog, we walk hand in hand with Jesus. We don't need to see into the future as long as we stay in touch with One who does. Our job is to keep moving.

Many people—even Christians—want to know the solution to their difficulty before they make their decision or begin their walk. That is not faith; that is sight. I like the way one of our lay leaders likes to describe Christian decision making: "Let's just walk in the Lord's direction as best we see it from here. When we get farther down the road, the turns will become obvious." Those who wait for the fog to lift will never get far. Others love the fog and know that "even the darkness will not be dark to You; the night will shine like the day, for darkness is as light to You" (Psalm 139:12).

Knock

Knocking implies persistence. The Lord loves persistence in prayer. One of the greatest prayer warriors of the Bible is Elijah. We read about him in James 5. The place was Mount Carmel, and the event was a showdown with the prophets of Baal. We all remember how Elijah mocked the Canaanites' feeble attempts to invoke Baal's power, and how he confidently called fire down on the Lord's altar after dousing it with precious water. But my favorite part of the story happens later, after everyone else has left the mountain.

The Bible tells us that Elijah climbed to the top of Carmel, bent down to the ground, and put his face between his knees in prayer. By means of prayer, Elijah asked God to put an end to a 3½-year drought. At first nothing happened. He told his servant to go and look toward the sea for any change in the weather. There was none. He told him to look again, but there was still no change. He sent his servant back seven times until he received the report: " 'A cloud as small as a man's hand is rising from the sea.' So Elijah said, 'Go and tell Ahab, "Hitch up your chariot and go down before the rain stops you" ' ." (1 Kings 18:44). And rain it did. Elijah was not easily discouraged. He kept knocking.

Is a Situation Standing between You and Serenity?

What unresolved situation calls for persistent prayer in your life? Elijah had his struggles too. When he felt that the miracle on Mount Carmel had no lasting impact on the hearts of Israel, Elijah gave up. He went out into the wilderness and asked God to take his life. He said he could not stand even one more day of apathy by God's people. The Lord heard Elijah's prayer of despair just the same as He heard his prayer of confidence that day on Mount Carmel. And the Lord again answered Elijah, but this time not the way Elijah requested. Instead of striking Elijah dead, God told him to quit whining and get back on the job. There were things to do and people to see.

God reminded Elijah that outcomes were His business, not Elijah's. Elijah had been wrong. He was not the only faithful person left in Israel. "I reserve seven thousand in Israel—all whose knees have not bowed down to Baal and all whose mouths have not kissed him" (1 Kings 19:18). His faith restored, Elijah went back to work.

God always answers the prayers of His children. The answer may not be the solution you were expecting, but He will answer. I like the way the New Testament tells us about the prayer life of Elijah. It says, "The prayer of a righteous man is powerful and effective. Elijah was a man just like us. He prayed earnestly that it would not rain, and it did not rain on the land for three and a half years. Again he prayed, and the heavens gave rain, and the earth produced its crops" (James 5:16–18).

Keep asking, seeking, and knocking. There was nothing special about Elijah; he was just like you. He had his ups and his downs, but Elijah's God—there's nothing He can't do. He can change situations.

Serenity Principle 6:
God Can Change Situations

Putting Principle 6 into Action

1. How have you seen God change situations that you thought were beyond anyone's ability to change?
   - Has any past miraculous event changed you in any way?
   - Describe that event and the impact it had on your life.
2. What situation needs changing in your life today?
   - Work through the 10 questions on pages 164-66 before attempting to make a change.
   - Do you still believe this is a change God wants to accomplish through you?
   - Write down what you feel is the best approach to the situation.
   - Pray about it daily for a week before beginning.

Pray Asking God to Help Change a Situation

Lord, I am confronted with a situation that won't go away by itself. I want to change it. Help me to check my motives and seek Your will in this matter. I need to gain some objectivity about this issue, Lord. Help me to see the situation as You see it. I know You will answer my call for help. I need renewal, redirection, and a reminder of Your love. Help me see all the other faithful Christians around me. Help me realize I am not alone. Restore to me the joy of your salvation and renew a proper spirit within me. Lord, go with me. Amen.

Principle 7

God's Word Is a Change Agent

How can we—limited by human inability—overcome our shortcomings, resist temptation, and break free from the slavery of sin? The first and best answer is by grace through faith in Jesus. He did what we can never do—lived the perfect life. By grace through faith in Him, we receive forgiveness of sins, and Christ's perfection becomes our own (see 2 Corinthians 5:21). But how do we overcome temptation and sin's destructive consequences?

No one will ever live a perfect life. Even Christians sin as Paul described so well in Romans 7:15–25. But the Bible offers hope to those who are weary of habitual sin and its consequences. God's Word is an agent for change. As trees rise above the brambles of a forest, Christians empowered by God's Word can break free from the slavery of sin.

Help

A tree is no better than its roots. Roots may seem insignificant compared to the great bulk of the tree. As a rule of thumb, roots represent only about 1/10th of the tree's mass. Appearances can be deceiving. Ask anyone who's ever removed a 50-year-old tree from his yard. The hairlike fibers in the root are as strong as any man-made cable. Cutting and splitting the tree's massive trunk is preferred to chopping out its root system. And a 50-year-old tree is a mere child compared to some species that routinely live hundreds or even thousands of years.[33]

Dendrochronologists are scientists who study the life cycle of trees. From studying the growth rings and scars of a tree, they are able to tell a great deal about its life. Some time ago it was necessary to fell a giant sequoia in California. After a detailed examination, the dendrochronologists made the following report.

> This sequoia was a seedling 271 years before Christ.
> 516 years later, that is 245 years after Christ, it was
> severely damaged by a forest fire. At once nature set to
> work to heal the wound by growing layers of living tissue
> over the gigantic scar left by the flames. In another
> century the wounds had been completely healed. In later
> years two more fires damaged the tree. The first of these
> had been entirely healed and the second was almost
> healed when the tree was finally cut down.[34]

Despite their massive size and ability to survive against incredible odds, trees are susceptible to infestation and disease. Trees that have survived hundreds of winters, severe ice storms, howling winds, and intense fires succumb to wood bores and beetles that slowly destroy their life-giving fibers from the inside out. Christians are no different. Many have overcome incredible odds, survived the death of a child, dealt with the loss of a spouse, endured the consequence of a tragic accident, or the effect of financial devastation. But even these people are not immune to the destructive nature of simple temptation. It starts innocently enough—just a look, only a thought, a mere deviation from the usual pattern. But there is no such thing as insignificant sin. The Bible compares those who toy with sin to the natural progression of any other relationship. James wrote, "Each one is tempted when, by his own evil desire, he is dragged away and enticed. Then, after desire has conceived, it gives birth to sin; and sin, when it is full-grown, gives birth to death. Don't be deceived, my dear brothers" (James 1:14–16). What begins as desire ends in death. Desire—enticement—conception—birth—life—growth—death; is the natural progression—unless the roots remain strong and healthy.

The Power of God Is in His Word

God's Word is power. That is why the psalmist can say that those who delight and meditate on God's Law are like a tree planted near good water (see Psalm 1:2–3). They will be productive (produce fruit), withstand the heat (their leaf does not wither), and prosper (live long). Those are characteristics everyone admires and desires. But how does the average person tap that power? Is it just a matter of knowing the Bible and applying biblical principles in your daily life?

Using the Bible is more than just the application of good advice. Truth is a powerful weapon in and of itself, but God's Word is more than truth. More than good advice? More than truth? What more can there be?

Unlike any other book, God's Word is a living thing. When it is used, God goes to work. The living nature of Scripture gives those who properly use it an incredible advantage over the power of sin and the devil. The Bible describes this power by saying, "The word of God is living and active. Sharper than any double-edged sword, it penetrates even to dividing soul and spirit, joints and marrow; it judges the thoughts and attitudes of the heart" (Hebrews 4:12). God's Word is sharper than any surgical knife and more accurate than any laser in identifying and eliminating the infestation of sin.

The Word of God is the only offensive weapon described in the long list of protective measures Christians can take when under spiritual assault by evil (see Ephesians 6:10–20). Paul called it "the sword of the Spirit, which is the word of God" (verse 17). After His Baptism, Jesus battled the devil in the wilderness. Although He was in every way God and in Him "all the fullness of the Deity lives in bodily form" (Colossians 2:9), Jesus voluntarily laid aside His divine powers and fought Satan in a manner that is just as effective for you and me. He used the Word. Every time Satan tempted Him, Jesus responded with Scripture.

- Although hungry and susceptible to the demands of His body, Jesus responded, "It is written: 'Man does not live on bread alone' " (Luke 4:4).

- Pride has been the downfall of many a great person, but when tempted by greatness, Jesus replied, "It is written: 'Worship the Lord your God and serve Him only' " (Luke 4:8).

- Those who withstand pride often fall prey to self-righteousness. But when the devil tempted Jesus to prove His faith by an act of daring, Jesus replied, "It says: 'Do not put the Lord your God to the test' " (Luke 4:12).

Satan is no match for the sword of the Lord, which is the Word of God. Jesus fought a spiritual battle with a spiritual weapon—the Word of God. And when confronted by God's powerful Word, the Bible tells us, "[Satan] left Him until an opportune time" (Luke 4:13).

Christians who've lost battles to temptation need new strategies. The solution to temptation is the same today as it was for Jesus. We can tell our enemies what Jeremiah was instructed to tell Egypt: " 'Take your positions and get ready, for the sword devours those around you.' Why will your warriors be laid low? They cannot stand, for the LORD will push them down. They will stumble repeatedly; they will fall over each other. They will say, 'Get up, let us go back to our own people and our native lands, away from the sword of the oppressor' " (Jeremiah 46:14–16).

Using the Power

The old saying "Those who fail to plan, plan to fail" is true. Christians without an intentional and spiritual game plan will fall prey to temptation every time. A good game plan is made of up three parts: a good defense, a good offense, and the resolve to win. Over the years many Christians under the oppression of some temptation or difficulty have come to me, defeated and disheartened. They have tried their best and failed. They no longer believe there is any hope for their cause—they have lost all courage.

Do you need a better sword for the battle? There is no greater weapon than the one God has fashioned for spiritual warfare—His Word. Everyone needs that help—even those "super-Christians" who appear to the rest of us ordinary, struggling Christians to be without doubts, trouble, or temptation. One of my favorite songs includes lines from a proverb of Solomon, "The name of the LORD is a strong tower; the righteous run to it and are safe" (Proverbs 18:10). Those who seem so secure have found the tower. Here's how you can find it too.

Develop Your Own Game Plan

Your game plan should be designed especially for you, using a specific "sword" designed to fight the enemy you are facing.

For years I have helped individuals develop a personal strategy to apply God's Word to a specific problem in their life. We forged a "sword" for use in battle against the specific temptation that Satan was using to trouble their life: alcohol abuse, nicotine addiction, a problem with food, anger, jealousy, pornography, greed, loneliness, depression ... you name it— they are legion. But, as Jesus showed in His own temptation, the devil is no match for God's Word. Together we found specific passages that countered their temptation and wrote them down. As Luther said in his famous hymn, "He [Satan] can harm us none, he's judged; the deed is done; one little word can fell him."[35] The devil *cannot* overcome a Christian armed with the Word of the Lord.

Make sure your "weapon" is always nearby—you don't know when the enemy might appear. Keep certain passages in your wallet, purse, or pocket just as a soldier keeps his weapon on his hip, ready for battle. When the temptation comes, the weapon is drawn and the enemy engaged. God's Word is not power in theory; it is power. It is the means by which He acts in your life to establish and bring about His will.

A Sample 'Weapon'

Use the following pages in your battle against temptation. Photocopy these pages and keep them in your wallet, purse, or datebook so they are accessible at any time.

Truth for the Moment of Temptation

1. **Your temptation is nothing new—others face it too.** "If you think you are standing firm, be careful that you don't fall! No temptation has seized you except what is common to man. And God is faithful; He will not let you be tempted beyond what you can bear. But when you are tempted, He will also provide a way out so that you can stand up under it" (1 Corinthians 10:12–13).

2. **You have a choice in the matter.** "Blessed is the man who perseveres under trial, because when he has stood the test, he will receive the crown of life that God has promised to those who love Him. When tempted, no one should say, 'God is tempting me.' For God cannot be tempted by evil, nor does He tempt anyone; but each one is tempted when, by his own evil desire, he is dragged away and enticed. Then, after desire has conceived, it gives birth to sin; and sin, when it is full-grown, gives birth to death. Don't be deceived" (James 1:12–16).

3. **God can rescue you from those who tempt you.** "The Lord knows how to rescue godly men from trials and to hold the unrighteous for the day of judgment. ... These men [our tempters] are springs without water and mists driven by a storm. Blackest darkness is reserved for them. For they mouth empty, boastful words and, by appealing to the lustful desires of sinful human nature, they entice people who are just escaping from those who live in error. They promise them freedom, while they themselves are slaves of depravity—for a man is a slave to whatever has mastered him. If they have escaped the corruption of the world by knowing our Lord and Savior Jesus Christ and are again entangled in it and overcome, they are worse off at the end than they were at the beginning. It would have been better for them not to have known the way of righteousness, than to have known it and then to turn their backs on the sacred command that was passed on to them. Of them the proverbs are true: 'A dog returns to its vomit,' and, 'A sow that is washed goes back to her wallowing in the mud' " (1 Peter 2:9, 17–22).

3. **More passages of truth for temptation:**
   - Even great Christian leaders suffered temptation (Romans 7:15–25).
   - God's strength is shown in our time of weakness (2 Corinthians 12:7–10).
   - We have power over sin because of our relationship to Jesus (Romans 6:3–7).
   - Jesus will pray for you and give you unbeatable strength (Romans 8:34, 37–39).
   - Don't trust your judgment, trust God's truth (Proverbs 3:5–6).
   - Pray, and remember your blessings (Philippians 4:4–9).

Help for the Moment of Temptation

1. **Jesus knows what it's like to be tempted and is ready to help.** "For surely it is not angels He helps, but Abraham's descendants. For this reason He had to be made like His brothers in every way, in order that He might become a merciful and faithful high priest in service to God, and that He might make atonement for the sins of the people. Because He Himself suffered when He was tempted, He is able to help those who are being tempted" (Hebrews 2:16–18).

2. **If you let Him, God can give you all the strength you need.** "Do you not know? Have you not heard? The LORD is the everlasting God, the Creator of the ends of the earth. He will not grow tired or weary, and His understanding no one can fathom. He gives strength to the weary and increases the power of the weak. Even youths grow tired and weary, and young men stumble and fall; but those who hope in the LORD will renew their strength. They will soar on wings like eagles; they will run and not grow weary, they will walk and not be faint" (Isaiah 40:28–31).

3. **Submit, resist, and succeed is God's formula for victory.** "Submit yourselves, then, to God. Resist the devil, and he will flee from you. Come near to God and He will come near to you. Wash your hands, you sinners, and purify your hearts, you double-minded. Grieve, mourn and wail. Change your laughter to mourning and your joy to gloom. Humble yourselves before the Lord, and He will lift you up" (James 4:7–10).

4. **Spend more time with God and less time with things that tempt you.** "Do not be deceived: God cannot be mocked. A man reaps what he sows. The one who sows to please his sinful nature, from that nature will reap destruction; the one who sows to please the Spirit, from the Spirit will reap eternal life. Let us not become weary in doing good, for at the proper time we will reap a harvest if we do not give up" (Galatians 6:7–9).

5. **Think about the consequence of temptation. You know better.** "Prepare your minds for action; be self-controlled; set your hope fully on the grace to be given you when Jesus Christ is revealed. As obedient children, do not conform to the evil desires you had when you lived in ignorance. But just as He who called you is holy, so be holy in all you do; for it is written: 'Be holy, because I am holy' " (1 Peter 1:13–16).

6. **More passages for help in temptation:**

   - The Holy Spirit will help you pray when the words don't come (Romans 8:26).
   - Jesus is ready and willing to ask the Father to help you (Hebrews 4:14–16).
   - Use the right weapons to fight the right enemy (Ephesians 6:10–20).
   - He gives help to the weary and strength to the weak (Matthew 11:28–30).
   - See the "big picture" and be thankful (Philippians 4:6–7).
   - Don't envy those who seem to get away with evil (Psalm 37).
   - You have been set free; slavery is broken (Romans 6:12–23).

Comfort for Those Who Have Fallen

1. **You are sinful and will make mistakes.** "He will not always accuse, nor will He harbor His anger forever; He does not treat us as our sins deserve or repay us according to our iniquities. For as high as the heavens are above the earth, so great is His love for those who fear Him; as far as the east is from the west, so far has He removed our transgressions from us. As a father has compassion on his children, so the LORD has compassion on those who fear Him; for He knows how we are formed, He remembers that we are dust" (Psalm 103:9–14).

2. **There is no God or person as gracious as the true God.** "Who is a God like You, who pardons sin and forgives the transgression of the remnant of His inheritance? You do not stay angry forever but delight to show mercy. You will again have compassion on us; You will tread our sins underfoot and hurl all our iniquities into the depths of the sea" (Micah 7:18–19).

3. **God's anger is short-lived, but His grace is new every morning.** "His anger lasts only a moment, but His favor lasts a lifetime; weeping may remain for a night, but rejoicing comes in the morning. When I felt secure, I said, 'I will never be shaken.' O LORD, when You favored me, You made my mountain stand firm; but when You hid Your face, I was dismayed. To You, O LORD, I called; to the Lord I cried for mercy" (Psalm 30:5–8).

4. **God heals and forgives. Stubborn fools make their own trouble.** "He who conceals his sins does not prosper, but whoever confesses and renounces them finds mercy. Blessed is the man who always fears the LORD, but he who hardens his heart falls into trouble" (Proverbs 28:13–14).

5. **God's Word is power. Use it.** "Let the wicked forsake his way and the evil man his thoughts. Let him turn to the LORD, and He will have mercy on him, and to our God, for He will freely pardon. 'For My thoughts are not your thoughts, neither are your ways My ways,' declares the LORD. 'As the heavens are higher than the earth, so are My ways higher than your ways and My thoughts than your thoughts. As the rain and the snow come down from heaven, and do not return to it without watering the earth and making it bud and flourish, so that it yields seed for the sower and bread for the eater, so is My word that goes out from My mouth: It will not return to Me empty, but will accomplish what I desire and achieve the purpose for which I sent it. You will go out in joy and be led forth in peace; the mountains and hills will burst into song before you, and all the trees of the field will clap their hands. Instead of the thornbush will grow the pine tree, and instead of briers the myrtle will grow' " (Isaiah 55:7–13).

6. **More passages of comfort when you've fallen:**

    - God is more forgiving than we are (Matthew 18:21–35).
    - When God forgives, He forgets (Isaiah 43:25).
    - Guilt has a solution (Psalm 32:1–7).

Pray for Help in Time of Need

A *prayer of* David

Hear, O LORD, *and answer me, for I am poor*
and needy. Guard my life, for I am devoted to You.
You are my God; save Your servant who trusts in You.
Have mercy on me, O Lord, for I call to You all day
long. Bring joy to Your servant, for to You, O Lord,
I lift up my soul. You are forgiving and good, O Lord,
abounding in love to all who call to You. Hear my
prayer, O LORD; *listen to my cry for mercy. In the*
day of my trouble I will call to You, for You will answer
me. Among the gods there is none like You, O Lord;
no deeds can compare with Yours. All the nations You
have made will come and worship before You, O Lord;
they will bring glory to Your name. For You are great
and do marvelous deeds; You alone are God. Teach me
Your way, O LORD, *and I will walk in Your truth; give*
me an undivided heart, that I may fear Your name.
I will praise You, O Lord my God, with all my heart;
I will glorify Your name forever. For great is Your love
toward me; You have delivered me from the depths of
the grave. The arrogant are attacking me, O God; a
band of ruthless men seeks my life—men without
regard for You. But You, O Lord, are a compassionate
and gracious God, slow to anger, abounding in love
and faithfulness. Turn to me and have mercy on me;
grant Your strength to Your servant and save the son
of Your maidservant. Give me a sign of Your goodness,
that my enemies may see it and be put to shame, for
You, O LORD, *have helped me and comforted me.*

(Psalm 86)

The Lord's Prayer

Our Father who art in heaven,
  Hallowed be Thy name,
  Thy kingdom come,
  Thy will be done
    on earth as it is in heaven.
Give us this day our daily bread;
and forgive us our trespasses
  as we forgive those
  who trespass against us;
and lead us not into temptation,
  but deliver us from evil.
For Thine is the kingdom
  and the power and the glory
  forever and ever. Amen.

Use these pages to help you move past *talking* about the power of God's Word to instead *using* the power of God's Word as Jesus did in His battle against the devil.

Jesus prayed a very specific and important prayer just before His arrest and crucifixion. He specifically said the prayer was for His disciples, but "not for them alone. I pray also for those who will believe in Me through their message" (John 17:20). That night He said, "My prayer is not that You take them out of the world but that You protect them from the evil one. They are not of the world, even as I am not of it. Sanctify them by the truth; Your word is truth" (John 17:15–17).

The serenity that comes from victory over temptation is achieved by the power of God's Word applied to the temptations of life. Jesus showed us how to use the Word, and He prayed that His Father would continue to keep us from evil by means of the same powerful weapon. God's Word is an agent for change. It will help you as you seek God's peace God's way.

Serenity Principle 7: God's Word Is a Change Agent

Putting Principle 7 into Action

1. Identify a temptation that troubles your life.
   - What passages in the examples provided are most helpful for you?
2. If you are struggling with some reccurring temptation, make a "sword" of your own by writing down Scripture passages that could help you gain a victory over your enemy.

- Post the passages where you will see them every day—in your car, on your dresser, on your desk at work.

Pray in Thanks for the Power of God's Word

Almighty Father, Giver of every good and perfect gift, daily I fall short of Your perfection. I want to do good, but despite my best intentions and sincere effort, I fail. Thank You, Lord, for Your rescue and the forgiveness You provide in Jesus. Thank You also for providing the weapon of Your Word to help me overcome my personal demons. Lord, help me to better understand how Your Word can help me overcome the temptations in my life. Help me to use my experience of Your grace to encourage and comfort others. Thank You, Lord. I pray in Jesus' name. Amen.

Principle 8

There Is Power in Prayer

L ike most people, I love Christmas. The good news of the Savior's birth is infectious. Traditions abound, all designed to bring people together in common expressions of love and good will. Certain hymns like "Silent Night" and "O Little Town of Bethlehem" have become an essential part of the Christmas Eve worship experience. Their enchanting melodies and poetic lyrics reflect the magic of that incredible night. Christian friends sing familiar carols before sitting down to their Christmas dinners. Others read the story of Jesus' birth from Luke's gospel before serving dessert.

I enjoy exchanging gifts, decorating the house, making cookies, Christmas caroling, and cold weather—all the sights, sounds, and smells of Christmas in America. The legends and stories of Christmas add to the celebration: *Frosty the Snowman, Ruldoph the Red-nosed Reindeer, The Little Drummer Boy,* and Santa Claus. Young children are captured each year by the imagery of Clement Moore's famous poem, "The Night before Christmas." Older children enjoy the prose of Charles Dickens' A *Christmas Carol.* The climax of Dickens' tale occurs when the Ghost of Christmas Yet to Come carries Scrooge to "a dismal, wretched, ruinous churchyard." The nightmare's purpose is revealed as Scrooge contemplates the inevitable outcome of his lifelong values.

> *The Spirit stood among the graves, and pointed down to One. He advanced towards it trembling. The Phantom was exactly as it had been, but he dreaded that he saw new meaning in its solemn shape.*

"Before I draw nearer to that stone to which you point," said Scrooge, "answer me one question. Are these the shadows of the things that Will be, or are they shadows of the things that May be, only?"

Still the Ghost pointed downward to the grave by which it stood.

"Men's courses will foreshadow certain ends, to which, if persevered in, they must lead," said Scrooge. "But if the courses be departed from, the ends will change. Say it is thus with what you show me!"

The Spirit was immovable as ever.

Scrooge crept towards it, trembling as he went; and following the finger, read upon the stone of the neglected grave his own name, EBENEZER SCROOGE.

"Am I that man who lay upon the bed?" he cried, upon his knees.

The finger pointed from the grave to him, and back again.

"No, Spirit! Oh no, no!"

The finger still was there.

"Spirit!" he cried, tight clutching at its robe, "Hear me! I am not the man I was. I will not be the man I must have been but for this intercourse. Why show me this, if I am past all hope?"

For the first time the hand appeared to shake.[36]

The question Scrooge asked is a question everyone must ask: "Are these the shadows of the things that *will be*, or are they shadows of the things that *may be* only?" Am I captive to the habits of my life? If, like Scrooge, I need to change, what action is required to alter my course and thus alter my life's outcome? As you may recall, Scrooge vowed to "honour Christmas in my heart, and try to keep it all the year. I will live in the Past, the

Present, and the Future. The Spirits of all three shall strive with me. I will not shut out the lessons they teach."[37] A fine resolve, but easier said than done. Old habits die hard.

Significant life change requires new thinking, beyond the ability of most people. We need help. Recovery groups offer hope; suddenly we are not alone, but it's a case of "good-news, bad-news." It's good to know others share our struggle, but it can be depressing to see how difficult it is to accomplish significant life change. Overcoming a detrimental lifestyle or achieving victory over a compulsive behavior takes more than a nightmare resulting in new resolve. It requires a completely new way of thinking, and for most people, help from a "higher power."

Finding Help in a 'Higher Power'

As the apostle Paul discovered in his travels, it is natural for people to believe in a "higher power." But what most believe as theory, Paul taught as fact: "Men of Athens! I see that in every way you are very religious. For as I walked around and looked carefully at your objects of worship, I even found an altar with this inscription: TO AN UNKNOWN GOD. Now what you worship as something unknown I am going to proclaim to you" (Acts 17:22–23). Paul knew what he was talking about. He had studied the ancient writings and had met the Lord face-to-face (see Acts 9). Paul would never forget that day on the road to Damascus. It was the day his life changed forever.

Before Paul met Jesus he was an aggressive, hard-charging, success-driven maniac. His pride and arrogance knew no limits. He once wrote, "If anyone else thinks he has reasons to put confidence in the flesh, I have more: circumcised on the

eighth day, of the people of Israel, of the tribe of Benjamin, a
Hebrew of Hebrews; in regard to the law, a Pharisee; as for
zeal, persecuting the church; as for legalistic righteousness,
faultless" (Philippians 3:4–6). Paul was on the fast track,
accomplishing more in less time than everyone else. He later
recalled, "I was advancing in Judaism beyond many Jews of my
own age and was extremely zealous for the traditions of my
fathers" (Galatians 1:14). But life can be cruel. What Paul
called success turned into sickness. In his search for happiness, he found hopelessness. Paul's freight train was about to
be derailed. But Jesus was waiting up ahead. Paul's path in life
was going to make a sharp turn—for the better.

A person's greatest need is to be significant, to be loved
and needed by another. In the search for significance, Jesus is
the destination. Paul gave up everything after meeting Jesus—
his status, his friends, his future, and eventually, even his life.
Did he consider it a loss? Just the opposite:

> *Whatever was to my profit I now consider loss for the sake
> of Christ. What is more, I consider everything a loss com-
> pared to the surpassing greatness of knowing Christ Jesus
> my Lord, for whose sake I have lost all things. I consider
> them rubbish, that I may gain Christ and be found in
> Him, not having a righteousness of my own that comes
> from the law, but that which is through faith in Christ—
> the righteousness that comes from God and is by faith."*
> *(Philippians 3:7–9)*

Finding God

Paul found God on the road to Damascus. (Actually God
did the finding; Paul was the findee.) Jesus also finds people
on the road to Denver, Detroit, Dallas, and all points throughout the world.

How hard is it to make the connection? Paul spoke from experience when he wrote, " 'Do not say in your heart, "Who will ascend into heaven?" ' (that is, to bring Christ down) 'or "Who will descend into the deep?" ' (that is, to bring Christ up from the dead). But what does it say? 'The word is near you; it is in your mouth and in your heart,' that is, the word of faith we are proclaiming. ... And Isaiah boldly says, 'I was found by those who did not seek me; I revealed myself to those who did not ask for me' " (Romans 10:6–8, 20).

Are you thinking, "But I'm not worth finding." Or "Why should He listen to me?" You're absolutely right. You aren't worth finding, and there is no reason He should listen to you, or to me, or to any other sinner. Now that you understand *grace*, you are ready to move on to other topics. Remember what Jesus told His followers: "Love your enemies and pray for those who persecute you, that you may be sons of your Father in heaven. He causes His sun to rise on the evil and the good, and sends rain on the righteous and the unright-eous. If you love those who love you, what reward will you get? Are not even the tax collectors doing that?" (Matthew 5:44–46). The fact that God loves you and cares what you think, say, and do is a measure of His *love*, not your worthi-ness. If you want to be like God, love those who least deserve it—people like you.

Why Pray?

Christians don't pray to keep God informed. Jesus said, "Are not two sparrows sold for a penny? Yet not one of them will fall to the ground apart from the will of your Father. And even the very hairs of your head are all numbered. So don't be afraid; you are worth more than many sparrows" (Matthew 10:29–31). God knows what you need before you ask

Him. He even knows what you are about to say before you say it. The psalmist reminds us, "Before a word forms on my tongue you know it completely, O LORD" (Psalm 139:4). So why do we pray?

I was raised by Christian parents who faithfully attended a Lutheran church in a small Indiana town. Growing up in a Christian home and attending a parochial school had its advantages—not fully appreciated during my childhood to be sure! One of those unappreciated values was memory work. We memorized not only the Ten Commandments, the Apostles' Creed, and the Lord's Prayer, but also Martin Luther's explanations to the Ten Commandments, the Apostles' Creed, and the Lord's Prayer. The explanation to the Fourth Petition of the Lord's Prayer made an impression on me, even as a child. Luther wrote, "God certainly gives daily bread to everyone without our prayers, even to all evil people, but we pray in this petition that God would lead us to realize this and to receive our daily bread with thanksgiving."[38] Christians don't pray to keep God informed. Prayer is an act of faith, commanded by God, who has promised to listen. Prayer connects us with the One who made the heaven and earth. There is power in prayer, not because of what we say, but because of God, who listens.

Prayer Changes Things and People

There are two ways to handle a bad situation: change the situation or change the person. Left to us, the answer to prayer would always be the same—change the situation. But God knows that difficulty is sometimes necessary in life. He knows how to change people. The expanded version of Reinhold Niebuhr's famous prayer acknowledges the place of adversity in accomplishing change:

God, grant me the serenity
To accept the things I cannot change,
Courage to change the things I can,
And the wisdom to know the difference,
Living one day at a time,
Enjoying one moment at a time,
Accepting hardship as a pathway to peace,
Taking, as Jesus did, the sinful world as it is,
Not as I would have it,
Trusting that You will make all things right
If I surrender to Your will,
So that I may be reasonably happy in this life
And supremely happy with You forever in the next.[39]

Prayer is not intended as an escape from reality. The Serenity Prayer acknowledges the reality of daily struggle with the words *accepting hardship as a pathway to peace, taking, as Jesus did, the sinful world as it is, not as I would have it.* The Lord can change situations as He did for the children of Israel in the days of Egypt's cruel oppression, but sometimes He chooses to change people and deepen their faith *through* their difficulties as He did for Job during his suffering at the hands of Satan. Having access to God through prayer does not mean all problems and troubles will disappear from the lives of the faithful. Jesus said, "I have told you these things, so that in Me you may have peace. In this world you will have trouble. But take heart! I have overcome the world" (John 16:33).

Letting God Be God

Which is more difficult for God: changing a bad situation or changing a person in a bad situation? Jesus raised that very question in a dialogue He had with some religious leaders. A paralyzed man was brought to Jesus for healing. Jesus said to the man, "Take heart, son; your sins are forgiven" (Matthew 9:2). Jesus chose to change the man. But there were some in the crowd who scoffed at His words, saying only God can forgive sins. Jesus, knowing their thoughts, asked, "Which is easier: to say, 'Your sins are forgiven,' or to say, 'Get up and walk'? But so that you may know that the Son of Man has authority on earth to forgive sins. ..." Then he said to the paralytic, 'Get up, take your mat and go home.' And the man got up and went home" (Matthew 9:5–7). The greatest miracles of God are not public displays of great power—calming storms, changing water into wine, healing the sick, or raising the dead—those things are easy for God. God's greatest miracles are displays of change in the lives of weak people.

Two artists were once asked to paint a picture illustrating serenity. The first painted a beautiful evening scene. In the foreground was a lake, its surface calm, surrounded by meadows that stretched as far as the eye could see. Cattle were gently grazing in the lush fields. Near the lake stood a small cottage, beautifully reflected in the quiet waters. The sun was setting, bathing the sky in shades of scarlet. Everything about the picture was serene.

The second artist chose a different path. He painted a wild, stormy scene with heavy black clouds rolling ominously overhead. Lightning flashed through the darkness as torrential rain lashed the setting. A raging river plunged over a high cliff in the center of the portrait, its waters crashing against the rocks in a never ending display of power. But nearby, in the shelter of a small crevice, a small bird sat secure on her nest, absolutely sheltered from the chaos that raged around her. The second painting depicted serenity better than the first. It was no contest. As Isaiah said of his God, "You will keep in perfect peace him whose mind is steadfast, because he trusts in You. Trust in the LORD forever, for the LORD, the LORD, is the Rock eternal" (Isaiah 26:3–4).

God cares about us. We are the ones who get hung up on situations. Left to us, the Christian life would always be tranquil like the first painting. But God knows that the power of peace within surpasses the value of peace without. There are others still living in the storm whom God desires to save. Christians must be near to offer them shelter. When His will is served, serenity is found, even in the storm. The Serenity Prayer includes this thought: *trusting that You will make all things right if I surrender to Your will.* Therein lies the key to serenity through prayer.

Prayer as an Act of Faith

People often get hung up on the mechanics of prayer. They develop elaborate rituals using candles, incense, the right intonations, fasting, and the right posture, but praying right is less important than right praying. Right praying requires faith in Jesus. You may know all the right words, understand the theology, and be able to quote the pertinent Scriptures, but unless prayers are offered through faith in Jesus, religious rituals are of no value. To be sure, the Lord hears the prayers of nonbelievers, just as He hears and knows all things. But only believers in Jesus can be absolutely certain their prayers will be quickly answered in a manner that seems best to God.

Jesus said, "I am the way and the truth and the life. No one comes to the Father except through Me" (John 14:6). That is not to say it is unimportant to learn all that the Bible teaches about prayer. It is, however, less important to know what the Bible says about prayer than it is to know the One who makes prayer possible.

Putting the Power of Prayer to Work

There's an old story about a recluse who was given a new chainsaw as a gift. He was thrilled. In eager anticipation, he hung his trusty old saw on the wall of the shed and oiled the blade of his new one. Cutting fuel for the wood-burning furnace was about to get easy. But his joy turned to frustration, then despair, and finally anger. No matter how hard he tried, the new saw just didn't cut as well as his trusty old crosscut. Reluctantly, he returned the saw to the store, making sure the salesman knew just how frustrated he was with all the empty promises. Puzzled by the complaint, the salesman gave the saw a thorough checkup then took it out back to try it out. With one pull on the cord the saw roared into action. But before he could lay the blade against the block of wood the "problem" became obvious when the recluse shouted, "What's that noise?!"

A chainsaw has incredible power provided its blades are sharp, it is filled with fuel, and its owner knows how to use it. Prayer is like that. Prayer is God's idea, encouraged by Him, and explained in His Word. Those who want to realize its full potential should consult the "owner's manual."

When You Pray

1. **Ask, don't tell.** Never forget God is God and you are not. Some people pray as though God were their own personal genie. They issue orders, believing the more firm they are in their "request," the more likely they will get their answer. Pray requests, not answers. "You ought to say, 'If it is the Lord's will, we will live and do this or that' " (James 4:15).

2. **Remember, God's power has no limit.** The Lord limits Himself only when love requires it. He cannot be coerced into doing anything detrimental to those He loves or to His

church. But nothing is too difficult for God. "No eye has seen, no ear has heard, no mind has conceived what God has prepared for those who love Him" (1 Corinthians 2:9). After Jesus calmed the wind and stilled the storm, His disciples were more afraid than before, and rightfully so. Mark tells us, "They were terrified and asked each other, 'Who is this? Even the wind and the waves obey Him!' " (Mark 4:41).

God often wants to do more even than our faith and abilities allow. His words to Moses as the children of Israel approached the Promised Land are telling. "I will not drive them out in a single year, because the land would become desolate and the wild animals too numerous for you. Little by little I will drive them out before you, until you have increased enough to take possession of the land" (Exodus 23:29–30). Could God have destroyed Israel's enemies quickly? No doubt about it. Why didn't He? He held back out of love and concern for the ability of Israel to handle His blessing.

3. **Talk in plain language.** Big words and flowery rhetoric may impress your mom while the turkey cools on Thanksgiving Day, but God is not your mom. Praying loud and long doesn't merit special attention from God. And, if it's done for show, Jesus said, "I tell you the truth, they have received their reward in full" (Matthew 6:5). Prayer is intended to be a heartfelt conversation between a child and his Father. Public prayers are not wrong and are even encouraged, but not at the expense of sincerity. Jesus went on to say, "When you pray, go into your room, close the door and pray to your Father, who is unseen. Then your Father, who sees what is done in secret, will reward you. And when you pray, do not keep on babbling like pagans, for they think they will be heard because of their many

words. Do not be like them, for your Father knows what you need before you ask Him" (Matthew 6:6–8).

4. **Be specific.** Pray what you mean and mean what you pray. Children who love their parents talk to their parents. Children of God who love their Lord talk to Him on a regular basis. Our heavenly Father wants His children to bring all their joys, sorrows, and needs to Him in prayer. "Do not be anxious about anything, but in everything, by prayer and petition, with thanksgiving, present your requests to God" (Philippians 4:6).

5. **Be confident.** God has asked you to pray and has promised to listen. When you pray, remember you are approaching God's throne of grace at His request. Be confident. "Call upon Me in the day of trouble; I will deliver you, and you will honor Me" (Psalm 50:15).

6. **Pray for others, even your enemies.** This may seem strange at first, but it makes perfect sense. God wants you to take all your troubles to Him. Some of those "troubles" come in the form of personal enemies. God advises, "Do not repay anyone evil for evil. Be careful to do what is right in the eyes of everybody. If it is possible, as far as it depends on you, live at peace with everyone. Do not take revenge, my friends, but leave room for God's wrath, for it is written: 'It is mine to avenge; I will repay,' says the Lord" (Romans 12:17–19). It may not be within your power to change problem people, but all things are possible for God.

Praying for others is high on God's list of expectations. By contrast, selfish prayers are a great offense to Him. The Bible says, "When you ask, you do not receive, because you ask with wrong motives, that you may spend what you get on your pleasures" (James 4:3). God cares too much to encourage selfishness by granting prayers that would be detrimental to His children in the long term. It is no accident that all the petitions of the Lord's Prayer include plural pronouns. Jesus modeled inclusive prayer.

7. **Prayer is not a solo act.** God not only graciously hears our prayers, He provides help for the "prayer challenged." Jesus is willing and well placed to make intercession for us. "Christ Jesus, who died—more than that, who was raised to life—is at the right hand of God and is also interceding for us" (Romans 8:34). (Hebrews 4:15–16 adds that Jesus speaks to the Father of our struggle from firsthand experience.) Not only does Jesus make intercession for us; the Holy Spirit makes *words* for us! "The Spirit helps us in our weakness. We do not know what we ought to pray for, but the Spirit himself intercedes for us with groans that words cannot express" (Romans 8:26).

8. **Pray continually.** Although long prayers cannot coerce God, He does invite the continued and persistent prayers of His children. I keep a list of prayer concerns in my monthly planner. Every day I review the list and pray for the people and situations written there. Concerns of more immediate importance are placed on each day's pages as a constant reminder.

Jesus encouraged persistence in prayer when He told the story of the unjust judge. "There was a widow in that town who kept coming to him with the plea, 'Grant me justice against my adversary.' For some time he refused. But finally he said to himself, 'Even though I don't fear God or care about men, yet because this widow keeps bothering me, I will see that she gets justice, so that she won't eventually wear me out with her coming!' And the Lord said, 'Listen to what the unjust judge says. And will not God bring about justice for His chosen ones, who cry out to Him day and night? Will He keep putting them off? I tell you, He will see that they get justice, and quickly' " (Luke 18:3–8).

9. **Visualize the people and situations as you pray**. I am often asked to pray in public, at board meetings, and in front of various influential people. In such settings, the devil loves to make Christians feel self-conscious. To remove all thoughts of yourself, visualize the situations and people for whom you are praying. When the devil tempted Jesus through Peter with selfish thoughts, Jesus rebuked him in the strongest possible way. "Get behind Me, Satan! You are a stumbling block to Me; you do not have in mind the things of God, but the things of men" (Matthew 16:23). When your mind is properly focused, distractions are much less likely.

10. **Pray to know God's Will.** A friend of mine likes to say he is praying less and less that God would bless his plans, and more and more to know *what* God is blessing. That's an excellent attitude for powerful prayer. It's the kind of prayer Jesus modeled in the Garden of Gethsemane: "Yet not My will, but Yours be done" (Luke 22:42). Is there power in prayer? Yes, incredible power. But like anything powerful, it must be used in a positive and constructive way. Knowing the will of God is the key to powerful prayer. John wrote, "This is the confidence we have in approaching God: that if we ask anything according to His will, He hears us. And if we know that He hears us—whatever we ask—we know that we have what we asked of Him" (1 John 5:14–15).

No Greater 'Potential' Power

Norman Vincent Peale once called prayer "the most powerful form of energy" because Christian prayer connects God's children to the resources of the One who made heaven and earth. Unfortunately, as Peale also observed, it is the most neglected of all solutions to humankind's problems. That "tragic omission," Peale wrote, "compels us to bear the entire weight and burden of life. Little wonder men break down, or fail to achieve the best possible [outcome]."[40] The result of such neglect is seen in the disheveled lives of too many Christians.

In our search for serenity, prayer is God's prescribed method of conquering those things we can't change. A child has never exhausted all her options until she asks her parents for help. A child of God has all the resources of the heavenly Father at her disposal. God gives His word on it: "The prayer of the righteous is powerful and effective" (James 5:16).

Serenity Principle 8: There Is Power in Prayer

Putting Principle 8 into Action

1. Develop the habit of recording prayer concerns in a place where you will see them routinely and be reminded to pray. If you want, divide your list into categories such as immediate needs, prayers of thanksgiving, ongoing concerns, and prayers for others.

   - As issues are resolved make sure to thank God for the outcome.
   - Let your prayers for others also remind you to show support through regular personal contact if possible.

2. Which of the 10 insights on prayer on pages 198-202
   seems most applicable to your situation? Why?

   • Write down the Bible passage recorded under that
     insight and keep it with your prayer list or post it
     in a visible place as a reminder.

Pray about Prayer

Lord, teach me how to pray and help me establish a better habit of prayer in my life. Help me be more faithful in praying for others. Thank You for the opportunity to talk to You without elaborate rituals. Thank You for listening and for responding with answers that have my best interest at heart. Grant my prayers according to Your will. And help me to accept Your will and be content. In Jesus' name. Amen.

Principle 9

It Is Not Good for Man to Be Alone

I grew up just across the tracks from Huntington College in Huntington, Indiana. The entire east end where we lived was riddled with quarries—some abandoned, others still actively worked for their limestone. Our favorite quarry was a place the locals called Lake Clare. It had been abandoned since the pumps could no longer keep pace with the natural springs that the cranes had uncovered. The water was ice cold and the quarry walls were steep.

We dove from the high ledges or jumped from trees that grew along the sheer banks. As long as you missed the "shore" there was never any danger of hitting bottom, more than 200 feet below the surface. Sometimes we grabbed large boulders and jumped off a ledge just to see how deep we could go before chickening out and breaking for the surface.

Lake Clare was a dangerous place. People often drowned there, including a cousin who lived just down the road from us. If too many people drowned in a given summer, someone posted "No Swimming" signs at the more dangerous spots, forcing people to use the section where your feet could touch bottom. It was supervised by lifeguards, but that cost money. Usually, we just rode our bikes to another quarry.

It was always important to swim with a buddy in the icy waters of Lake Clare. If you got a cramp or hypothermia, a friend could toss you an inner tube or grab hold of your shirt (we always wore shirts as protection against the cold) and pull you out. My older brother once paralyzed half his face by diving straight into the icy waters after a day of baling hay in the hot summer sun. It was a week before he could drink from a cup without dribbling down his chin!

The Risk Factor

A rite of passage for a Huntington teenager was swimming across Lake Clare. It was a worthy challenge that took no small amount of courage. The lake was 300–400 yards across and three times as long. Once a swimmer started across, there was no stopping—it was all or nothing. For safety, we swam across in packs of three or four with someone paddling an inner tube. The encouragement of having someone nearby was important.

There is something about human nature that draws strength from companionship. It is the way God made us.

It takes courage to achieve significant personal change. Success comes easier with the encouragement of others. As teenagers, we never made anyone swim across the lake if they didn't want to, and some chose not to. Personal change comes from a willing heart, not by compulsion. Every situation presents at least two options: You can stay in the shallow end, where the lifeguards sit and your feet can touch, or you can jump in over your head and swim for it. There are consequences and a degree of uncertainty either way. What will happen if you embrace change? What will happen if you don't?

Change, by definition, requires risk. You have to move beyond the ropes of your present routine and push out into deep water. You can limit the risk but never completely eliminate it. Helen Keller said it well: "Security is mostly a superstition. It does not exist in nature, nor do the children of men as a whole experience it. Avoiding danger is no safer in the long run than outright exposure. Life is either a daring adventure or nothing."[41] To keep from drowning, you will need a buddy or two. In the days of my youth, I swam with friends who could pull me out or toss me a float. I still do.

One Is the Loneliest Number

Long before the term *sociology* was coined, the Lord declared a simple truth about the nature of man. He observed, "It is not good for man to be alone" (Genesis 2:18).

The Genesis account tells us that God made man on the sixth day as the crowning glory of His creation. Not even the angels were created to receive greater honor. The Bible describes those heavenly beings as "ministering spirits sent to serve those who will inherit salvation" (Hebrews 1:14). But there was trouble in paradise. Not the kind that comes from something forgotten or left undone. No, this was the kind of trouble permitted by a parent to teach a child an important lesson through self-discovery. God had made every animal male and female except for man. Adam was all alone with no other created thing exactly like him. There was no female human.

The Lord began the lesson. He brought all the animals to Adam to see what he would name them. And whatever Adam named them, that was their name. But something more important than name-calling was going on that day. When all was said and done, the Bible tells us, "But for Adam no suitable helper was found" (Genesis 2:20). God's plan was deliberate. He had not forgotten Adam's need for a companion. Knowing man's self-sufficient spirit, God wanted Adam to discover his great need for companionship before supplying the perfect solution—one God had intended from the start. And so the

Lord caused Adam to fall into a deep sleep and, while Adam slept, the Lord created just the right companion for him. The bond was like no other. Adam said, "This is now bone of my bones and flesh of my flesh; she shall be called 'woman,' for she was taken out of man" (Genesis 2:23).

The Value of Companionship

Man was made to live in relationship with other people. Not everyone is made for marriage, the most intimate of relationships, but a healthy life is connected to other people. Man was not made to be alone. Solomon described the pain of loneliness:

> There was a man all alone; he had neither son nor brother. There was no end to his toil, yet his eyes were not content with his wealth. "For whom am I toiling," he asked, "and why am I depriving myself of enjoyment?" This too is meaningless—a miserable business! Two are better than one, because they have a good return for their work: If one falls down, his friend can help him up. But pity the man who falls and has no one to help him up! Also, if two lie down together, they will keep warm. But how can one keep warm alone? Though one may be overpowered, two can defend themselves. A cord of three strands is not quickly broken.   (Ecclesiastes 4:8–12)

Let's look more closely at Solomon's reasons for companionship:

1. **Without someone who cares, success is meaningless—Solomon called it "miserable business."** Anyone who travels alone has experienced in a small way what Solomon is describing. Eating the finest fare alone is less enjoyable than sharing an inferior meal with a friend. I recently traveled to northern Russia to encourage our mis-

sionaries and their families working there. It was in the middle of winter and the beauty of the scenery in the eerie northern light was hard to describe to Carol back home. When we talked on the phone or I sent e-mail, I found myself repeating, "I wish you could be here. I wish you could see this." Experiences and achievements are meant to be shared with others who care about us. The old maxim is true: "A joy shared is a joy multiplied, but a trouble shared is trouble divided."

2. **Two get more done**. Solomon said they have a good return for their work. This is the same principle that allows swimmers or runners the energy to surpass their normal limits when a companion is alongside. Although there is no obvious physical explanation, cooperation has a psychological impact that results in increased ability. Studies show cooperation has an exponential effect on outcomes, greater than simple addition. One expert qualified the effect by saying, "Cooperation increases efficiency in amazing proportions. Two working together in perfect agreement have five-fold the efficiency of the same two working separately."[42]

In his book *Developing Leaders around You*, John Maxwell makes the same point through a story out of our rural past. "At a Midwestern fair, many spectators gathered for an old fashioned horse pull (an event where various weights are put on a horse-drawn sled and pulled along the ground). The grand champion horse pulled a sled with 4,500 pounds on it. The runner-up was close, with a 4,400 pound pull. Some of the men wondered what the two horses could pull if hitched together. Separately the weight they pulled totaled nearly 9,000 pounds, but when hitched and working together as a team, they pulled over 12,000 pounds!"[43] The increased capacity of the two working together was one-third greater than the combined effort of each individually. There is strength in unity.

3. **Two can help each other through hard times.** Solomon said, *If one falls down, his friend can help him up. But pity the man who falls and has no one to help him up*! When tackling personal change or overcoming the adverse effects of an unforeseen setback, a companion is essential. We all fail. How we handle failure will determine the degree of our success. Having a friend to help you through the hard times can make the critical difference.

4. **Companionship means comfort.** Did you ever try to build a fire with only one stick? It can't be done. Even a raging fire quickly dies if the logs are separated. They need each other to survive. The same is true with people. The world can be a cold and cruel place. *If two lie down together, they will keep warm. But how can one keep warm alone*?

5. **A friend is your best defense.** Have you ever taught a 16-year-old to drive in city traffic? It's not a pleasant experience. They have no understanding of the blind spot. All those years as passengers, they enjoyed the freedom of looking in any and every direction—in front, alongside, or even behind the car. The view from the driver's seat is decidedly different. Good drivers keep their eyes on the road, glancing from time to time at the sideview mirrors. Experienced drivers know the mirrors aren't enough. There are blind spots that require extreme caution. An extra set of eyes can help, especially when a driver wants to merge onto the interstate or change lanes in traffic. Life is like that. You will never see every danger, but an extra pair of eyes can help. We all have blind spots. It may be a flaw in our character or a temptation lying in wait. Everyone is vulnerable to something. An extra set of eyes can help protect you.

6. **There is strength in numbers.** I love challenging children to seemingly simple but impossible tasks. Try inviting a teenager to grab a dollar bill from your fingers as you drop it to the ground. Place the bill vertically between your thumb and finger. Have the teen position her parted fingers in the same way just below yours, ready to grab the bill as soon as you let go. You might even demonstrate how easily the dollar can be snagged by letting go with one hand and grabbing it with the other. The difference of course is that your mind will automatically tell your waiting hand when to react and you'll grab it every time. The teen, on the other hand, will never be able to catch the dollar as it floats through her fingers to the ground below. The reaction time required for eye/hand coordination is too great. It's a physiological impossibility. It's also a good way to teach children about the danger of overconfidence.

A similar lesson involves a straw and a long nail or spike. Invite any child who thinks he can bend the straw to come forward and give it a try. (I like to demonstrate just how easily a straw can be bent by twisting and tying it into knots as I talk.) As the child comes forward, slip the spike in the straw and hand it to him. He will never be able to bend, break, or tie that fortified straw into knots. "Unfair," he'll claim. "You cheated me. You put a nail inside the straw when I wasn't looking!" He is now ready to learn an important lesson about the way God made people. Left alone, we are vulnerable, easily twisted, turned, and defeated. But there is strength in numbers. *Though one may be overpowered, two can defend themselves. A cord of three strands is not quickly broken.*

The demonstration can also be done with three pencils. Ask a child if he thinks he is strong enough to break a simple pencil. Show how easily it can be done while you talk. Then, just before you give your volunteer the opportunity, wrap three pencils together with rubber bands! "Not fair!" he'll say. Solomon demonstrated the same truth with three cords. A small cord can be easily broken but, braided together, vulnerable things become invulnerable. One of the ways God strengthens people is by joining one to the strength of others.

The Power of Encouragement

It's hard to overstate the importance of encouragement. One of my favorite stories on the subject happened in Morris, Minnesota, in the early 1960s. It is best told in the words of a teacher who, because of a frustrating day in math class, taught a much more important lesson on the power and importance of encouragement. Sister Helen P. Mrosla likes to call her story "All the Good Things."

> He was in the first third grade class I taught at Saint Mary's School in Morris, MN. All 34 of my students were dear to me, but Mark Eklund was one in a million. He was very neat in appearance but had that happy-to-be-alive attitude that made even his occasional mischievousness delightful. Mark talked incessantly. I had to remind him again and again that talking without permission was not acceptable. What impressed me so much, though, was his sincere response every time I had to correct him for misbehaving—"Thank you for correcting me, Sister!" I didn't know what to make of it at first, but before long I became accustomed to hearing it many times a day.
>
> One morning my patience was growing thin when Mark talked once too often, and then I made a novice teacher's mistake. I looked at him and said, "If you say

one more word, I am going to tape your mouth shut!" It wasn't ten seconds later when Chuck blurted out, "Mark is talking again." I hadn't asked any of the students to help me watch Mark, but since I had stated the punishment in front of the class, I had to act on it. I remember the scene as if it had occurred this morning. I walked to my desk, very deliberately opened my drawer and took out a roll of masking tape. Without saying a word, I proceeded to Mark's desk, tore off two pieces of tape and made a big X with them over his mouth. I then returned to the front of the room. As I glanced at Mark to see how he was doing he winked at me. That did it! I started laughing. The class cheered as I walked back to Mark's desk, removed the tape and shrugged my shoulders. His first words were, "Thank you for correcting me, Sister."

At the end of the year I was asked to teach junior high math. The years flew by, and before I knew it Mark was in my classroom again. He was more handsome than ever and just as polite. Since he had to listen carefully to my instructions in the "new math," he did not talk as much in ninth grade as he had in the third. One Friday, things just didn't feel right. We had worked hard on a new concept all week, and I sensed that the students were frowning, frustrated with themselves—and edgy with one another. I had to stop this crankiness before it got out of hand. So I asked them to list the names of the other students in the room on two sheets of paper, leaving a space between each name. Then I told them to think of the nicest thing they could say about each of their classmates and write it down. It took the remainder of the class period to finish the assignment, and as the students left the room, each one handed me the papers. Charlie smiled. Mark said, "Thank you for teaching me, Sister. Have a good weekend."

That Saturday, I wrote down the name of each student on a separate sheet of paper, and I listed what everyone else had said about that individual. On Monday I gave each student his or her list. Before long, the entire class was smiling. "Really?" I heard whispered. "I never knew that meant anything to anyone!" "I didn't know others liked me so much!" No one ever mentioned those papers in class again. I never knew if they discussed them after class or with their parents, but it didn't matter. The exercise had accomplished its purpose. The students were happy with themselves and one another again. That group of students moved on.

Several years later, after I returned from vacation, my parents met me at the airport. As we were driving home, Mother asked me the usual questions about the trip—the weather, my experiences in general. There was a light lull in the conversation. Mother gave Dad a sideways glance and simply said, "Dad?" My father cleared his throat as he usually did before something important. "The Eklunds called last night," he began. "Really?" I said. "I haven't heard from them in years. I wonder how Mark is." Dad responded quietly. "Mark was killed in Vietnam," he said. "The funeral is tomorrow, and his parents would like it if you could attend." To this day I can still point to the exact spot on I-494 where Dad told me about Mark.

I had never seen a serviceman in a military coffin before. Mark looked so handsome, so mature. All I could think at that moment was, Mark, I would give all the masking tape in the world if only you would talk to me. The church was packed with Mark's friends. Chuck's sister sang "The Battle Hymn of the Republic." Why did it have to rain on the day of the funeral? It was difficult enough at the graveside. The pastor said the usual *prayers, and the bugler played "Taps." One by one those who loved Mark took a last walk by the coffin and sprinkled it with holy water.*

I was the last one to bless the coffin. As I stood there, one of the soldiers who had acted as pallbearer came up to me. "Were you Mark's math teacher?" he asked. I nodded as I continued to stare at the coffin. "Mark talked about you a lot," he said. After the funeral, most of Mark's former classmates headed to Chuck's farmhouse for lunch. Mark's mother and father were there, obviously waiting for me. "We want to show you something," his father said, taking a wallet out of his pocket. "They found this on Mark when he was killed. We thought you might recognize it." Opening the billfold, he carefully removed two worn pieces of notebook paper that had obviously been taped, folded and refolded many times. I knew without looking that the papers were the ones on which I had listed all the good things each of Mark's classmates had said about him. "Thank you so much for doing that," Mark's mother said. "As you can see, Mark treasured it." Mark's classmates started to gather around us. Charlie smiled rather sheepishly and said, "I still have my list. It's in the top drawer of my desk at home." Chuck's wife said, "Chuck asked me to put his in our wedding album." "I have mine too," Marilyn said. "It's in my diary." Then Vicki, another classmate, reached into her pocketbook, took out her wallet, and showed her worn and frazzled list to the group. "I carry this with me at all times," Vicki said without batting an eyelash. "I think we all saved our lists."

That's when I finally sat down and cried. I cried for Mark and for all his friends who would never see him again.[44]

Encouragement matters.

Friends Hold You Accountable

The term *friend* means lots of different things. One of the important implications is honesty. A friend speaks the truth in love. A friend cares enough to get involved even if it means telling the truth to people who would prefer a lie.

King David was a great leader of God's people. God loved his heart, his passion, and his honesty. David was also a sinner. Who hasn't heard the famous story of Bathsheba? Was she bathing on the roof hoping to attract the attention of the king, or did it all happen accidentally? Based on what we know about the people involved, we must assume it was unintentional on both parts. Whatever the reason, after David noticed Bathsheba, he was as James describes, "tempted by his own evil desire, ... dragged away and enticed" (James 1:14). The potential for serious consequences was great. David's kingdom, his life, even his very soul was in jeopardy. To make matters worse, Bathsheba became pregnant.

The problem did not seem insurmountable. After all, Bathsheba was a married woman whose husband was away on military assignment. The solution was simple. David could order Bathsheba's husband home and let nature take its course. A soldier separated from his wife for such a long time would certainly reconsummate their relationship, the adultery would be covered, and life would return to normal. But David had not counted on the integrity of Bathsheba's husband, Uriah, whose ethical standards would not allow him to enjoy the comforts of home while his fellow soldiers were still in harm's way. Although we can assume David and Bathsheba did all they could to break the soldier's resolve, his convictions surprised them both. As long as his regiment was on the battlefield, Uriah would sleep only in the military barracks.

Despite the king's permission, Uriah would not violate his pledge to the troops.

> Uriah said to David, "The ark and Israel and Judah
> are staying in tents, and my master Joab and my lord's
> men are camped in the open fields. How could I go to my
> house to eat and drink and lie with my wife? As surely
> as you live, I will not do such a thing!" (2 Samuel 11:11)

David resorted to plan B. If Uriah could not be tempted by lust, perhaps he could be persuaded through drink. He asked the soldier to remain one more night before returning to his company. The king plied Uriah with alcohol until he became drunk. But drunk or sober, faithful Uriah refused to sleep with his wife. There were only two choices left for the king: allow Bathsheba's adultery to be discovered or make sure it didn't matter.

> David wrote a letter to Joab [his commander] and sent
> it with Uriah. In it he wrote, "Put Uriah in the front line
> where the fighting is fiercest. Then withdraw from him
> so he will be struck down and die." So while Joab had the
> city under siege, he put Uriah at a place where he knew
> the strongest defenders were. When the men of the city
> came out and fought against Joab, some of the men in
> David's army fell; moreover, Uriah the Hittite died.
> (2 Samuel 11:14–17)

Sin's simple but deadly progression is clearly demonstrated in the story of David and Bathsheba. Before all was said and done their indiscretion led to death. I wonder how David felt when he handed Uriah his own death sentence, commanding him to deliver it to Joab? How did Joab react when he read the strange orders faithful Uriah delivered? Did the general watch Uriah fall in battle? How did he convince the other soldiers to let one of their own die? Do you think

David ever told Bathsheba that her husband was murdered? If he did, how could she ever love David or live with her guilt? If he kept the decision a secret, how could he go on pretending? How could Joab order the death of a faithful soldier just to please an immoral king? It's enough to drive a person crazy, and might have—except for the intervention of a friend.

The Bible tells us the Lord sent Nathan to blow the cover off David's lies. By telling a story about a poor man whose only lamb was stolen and killed by a rich man, Nathan helped David acknowledge his sin of adultery and murder. David deserved death, but he confessed his sin and God spared his life. David and Bethsheba married. Their newborn son became very ill and died seven days after he was born. It's a tragic story, but the Lord is also a God of mercy and compassion. David and Bathsheba conceived a second baby who God nicknamed "Jedidiah." Nathan, the same prophet who had confronted David, announced God's renewed favor. The baby's nickname meant "beloved by the Lord," but the rest of the world called him Solomon, king of Israel.

How important was the confrontation of Nathan in the life of David? It saved the king's life. More important, it restored his soul. David explained it this way:

> Blessed is he whose transgressions are forgiven,
> whose sins are covered. Blessed is the man whose sin
> the LORD does not count against him and in whose spirit
> is no deceit. When I kept silent, my bones wasted away
> through my groaning all day long. For day and night
> Your hand was heavy upon me; my strength was sapped
> as in the heat of summer. Then I acknowledged my sin
> to You and did not cover up my iniquity. I said, "I will
> confess my transgressions to the LORD"—and You
> forgave the guilt of my sin.   (Psalm 32:1–5)

Through David's confession—prompted by God—and the Lord's compassion, David's guilt was lifted. We each need the grace of God and a faithful friend to guide our wayward feet back to solid ground. That's what Christian friends are for: "Remember this: Whoever turns a sinner from the error of his way will save him from death and cover over a multitude of sins" (James 5:20).

One of the positive results of the Promise Keepers movement in America has been the establishment of intentional accountability groups among Christian friends. The Bible says, "As iron sharpens iron, so one man sharpens another" (Proverbs 27:17). That counsel of Solomon is applied in a very practical way as men are encouraged to seek an older friend as a mentor (a Paul), a peer as a companion (a Barnabas), and a younger man to nurture and encourage (a Timothy). This is not a new concept for those who've participated in recovery groups of various kinds. What has worked for those overcoming destructive, compulsive behaviors is now being applied successfully by Christians facing the day-to-day stress of life: friends helping friends as the Lord intended.

When we swam in the quarries of Indiana, the buddy system was necessary for safety. A friend was always nearby to help. These days, I participate in a breakfast meeting each week with men who keep me safe in more important ways. We study the Bible and ask each other tough questions like those listed below. We talk honestly about our lives and pray for each other and for each other's families. The waters of life can be cold and deep. The pressure at these depths can sap your strength and distort reality. Having a Christian friend nearby can be the difference between life and death. Friends can guide your feet back to the path of peace, the path of serenity. Make sure you always have a buddy nearby.

10 Questions for Greater Accountability

1. Did you accomplish your personal physical goals this week?
2. Did you accomplish your personal spiritual goals this week?
3. Did you spend time in prayer and Bible study every day this week?
4. Did you spend time praying for other members of this group?
5. What lesson is God teaching you this week?
6. What sin has plagued you this week?
7. How did you compromise your integrity? How did you deal with it?
8. Are you pleasing God with the way you use your money?
9. What did you do to show your spouse and family your love this week?
10. Did you have a Bible study and prayer time with your spouse/family this week?

Serenity Principle 9: It Is Not Good for Man to Be Alone

Putting Principle 9 into Action

1. When were you at your loneliest?
   - What about that situation caused you to feel isolated from others?
   - How did that situation resolve?
   - What are some of the lessons you learned through that experience?
2. Try using Sister Helen Mrosla's idea in a group.

- Prepare a sheet with everyone's name on it, allowing enough space for each member to write one or two positive descriptive comments.
- Collect the sheets and record all the positive information about each person on a single sheet that you can distribute at your next meeting.
- You may want to read Sister Mrosla's story or use Philippians 4:8–9 and Hebrews 10:23–25 as devotional thoughts before explaining the process.

3. Who holds you spiritually accountable?
   - Is there anyone in your circle of close friends who would have permission to ask you the types of questions listed on page 220?
   - If such a group doesn't already exist, consider forming a small group for the purpose of Bible study, prayer, and accountability. At first, agree only to meet for three months. At the end of that time, revisit the value of such an experience in your life and in the lives of the participants. Then decide if the group should continue meeting.

Pray about the Value of Friendship

Lord, You know how much I need friends. But I'm a sinful person, and sometimes I'm tempted to withdraw and go it alone. I know that's not a healthy attitude. Help me be a friend to others. Be glorified in my life and my relationships, Lord. Through me uplift, sustain, and encourage others. Help me as You helped David. Show me the destructive nature of my sin and the extent of Your compassion. Help me turn from what is wrong, trusting You for the strength to overcome the sin that so easily entangles me. In Your love and in Jesus' name I put my trust. Amen.

Principle 10

Eliminating Negatives Is Not Enough

Complete freedom from unwanted behavior requires that the Lord have complete access to your heart. Paul urged first-century Christians to cling to the faith of their Baptism. He said, "Let us draw near to God with a sincere heart in full assurance of faith, having our hearts sprinkled to cleanse us from a guilty conscience and having our bodies washed with pure water. Let us hold unswervingly to the hope we profess, for He who promised is faithful" (Hebrews 10:22–23). The weeds that ruin lives are called sin. They were destroyed on the cross at great cost to the Father. He did not spare even the life of His own Son but sacrificed Him to set us free. We can be confident He will give us all we need to sustain our new life.

Four-star General Charles Krulak is a United States Marine Corps Commandant. He has noticed something about American youth that many seem to have missed: Their lives are out of order and they're looking for direction in all the wrong places. When positive direction is lacking, any direction will do and young people won't sit idle for long.

"Today's youth," Krulak contends, "rather than fitting the slacker stereotype, are actually looking for something to believe in and to belong to. Unfortunately, often all society offers them is a gang. The gang gives them standards. They are part of a big institution that they're proud of. The culture is not meeting their needs. We are not giving them standards."[45]

General Krulak understands that eliminating negatives is not enough. It's not enough to tell young people, "Say no to drugs." We must address the need that is driving them to drugs. Krulak believes many are searching for significance and acceptance. The Marines, he asserts, is the perfect answer to those wanting to stand out from the crowd. Instead of lowering the standards, General Krulak has raised the expectations: "You will not see an advertisement that says anything about a college fund. You will not see one that says we will give you a skill. All we say is, do you want to be challenged physically, mentally and morally? Join the Marine Corps, and we'll guarantee you'll be changed, and the change will be forever. That's our commercial."[46]

The general's method is built on sound precedent. Jesus recruited using much the same strategy. Luke describes it in his account of the Lord's public life.

> As they were walking along the road, a man said to
> Him, "I will follow You wherever you go." Jesus replied,
> "Foxes have holes and birds of the air have nests,
> but the Son of Man has no place to lay His head."
> He said to another man, "Follow Me." But the man
> replied, "Lord, first let me go and bury my father."
> Jesus said to him, "Let the dead bury their own
> dead, but you go and proclaim the kingdom of God."
> Still another said, "I will follow You, Lord; but first
> let me go back and say good-bye to my family." Jesus
> replied, "No one who puts his hand to the plow and
> looks back is fit for service in the kingdom of God."
> (Luke 9:57–62)

Jesus didn't offer ease of life to those He met along the way. He offered significance. Christian ministries that seek to attract people to Christ by meeting "felt needs" must be careful not to overlook a person's greatest need—the need for acceptance and significance. Both are found in Jesus Christ. He didn't invite His disciples to follow Him into a life of ease. He said, " 'Come, follow Me, ... and I will make you fishers of men.' At once they left their nets and followed Him" (Mark 1:17–18). He challenged them to accept a life of sacrifice that was worthy of their time.

A life of serenity is not synonymous with a life of ease. God created people to be productive. Even before sin, the Bible tells us "The LORD God took the man and put him in the Garden of Eden to work it and take care of it" (Genesis 2:15). Work was *not* God's curse for sin—pain, hardship, and death were. Even the consequence of sin is used by God to drive us back to Him. Otherwise, through continued disobedience, we would stray from our one and only source of salvation. Continued dependence on the Lord is a strength, not a weakness:

> Two things I ask of You, O LORD; do not refuse me
> before I die: Keep falsehood and lies far from me;
> give me neither poverty nor riches, but give me only
> my daily bread. Otherwise, I may have too much and
> disown you and say, "Who is the LORD?" Or I may
> become poor and steal, and so dishonor the name
> of my God. (Proverbs 30:7–9)

There Is No Such Thing as Neutral Ground

When it comes to sin that dominates and controls life against our will, Jesus told an important story. It's a story that reminds us *it is not enough to eliminate negative behavior.* Permanent change requires that Christ take up permanent residence in your heart and life.

> He who is not with me is against me, and he who
> does not gather with me, scatters. When an evil
> spirit comes out of a man, it goes through arid
> places seeking rest and does not find it. Then it
> says, "I will return to the house I left." When it
> arrives, it finds the house swept clean and put in
> order. Then it goes and takes seven other spirits
> more wicked than itself, and they go in and live
> there. And the final condition of that man is worse
> than the first.   (Luke 11:23–26)

Those who have attempted change and experienced failure are less likely to attempt change again. As Jesus described, their final condition is worse than the first. They have learned that sincere effort and heartfelt resolve are not enough. They realize the truth about the enemy as described in Serenity Principle 2: Expect Opposition. They know the truth of Paul's warning: "Our struggle is not against flesh and blood, but against the rulers, against the authorities, against the powers of this dark world and against the spiritual forces of evil in the heavenly realms" (Ephesians 6:12). Those who have tried and failed know that it is not enough to eliminate wrong behavior from life. They must discover the reason for the wrong behavior. It's not enough to decide that smoking, compulsive eating, uncontrolled anger, substance abuse, cursing, gossip, lying, and stealing are undesirable. The first step toward victory is to ask *why* you practice those undesirable behaviors. What purpose do they serve in your life? What pain, stress, or difficulty is driving you to self-destruction? Then you can seek the counsel of the Lord and gain the benefit of His Word in that area of your life. Then you can use the biblical principles outlined here to gain the victory.

Turning a Bad Situation Around

Life doesn't have to be a downward spiral toward destruction. The power of light is greater than darkness. Whenever light, no matter how small, enters a room, darkness is overpowered. Richard Rhodes is living proof of this important principle. Dr. Rhodes has written 10 books and received the Pulitzer Prize and the National Book Award for his 1987 book *The Making of the Atomic Bomb*. The story behind Dr. Rhodes' success might surprise you.

When he was only 13 months old, his mother killed herself. She was only 29 years old. In his book *A Hole in the World: An American Boyhood*, Dr. Rhodes recounts an incredible life of abuse and neglect that should have destroyed him and his older bother, Stanley. Richard's father was an engine mechanic for the Missouri-Pacific Railroad, a job that didn't allow much time for parental supervision. For the first six years of his life, Richard lived in a boardinghouse near the railroad yards in Kansas City. His early years were more or less supervised by a very kind and loving immigrant couple from Germany who owned the apartment where the Rhodes lived. During his 10th summer, Richard's father remarried. A worse nightmare could not be imagined.

> *Our new stepmother, a woman from an impoverished Texas mining background named Anne Martin, proved to be as remorselessly cruel as the worst stepmothers of folklore. For two and a half years, Stanley and I suffered through a nightmare of extreme child abuse. We were slapped and kicked, beaten with belt buckles and spike-heeled shoes, denied the use of a toilet at night, denied access to a bathtub or shower for as much as a month at a time, put out to long hours of work collecting soft-drink bottles for their deposits and selling notions from door to door,*

and sent outdoors in thin rags on weekends to wander the
streets from morning to night in sub-zero weather.

Worst of all, we were deliberately starved. While she
and Dad enjoyed a regular diet that included steak and
fresh fruit, our stepmother boiled up a pot of black-eyed
peas without salt or seasoning for us once a week. Burned
black-eyed peas mashed to bitter gruel and burned, some-
times rotten, hard-boiled eggs constituted most of our diet
… my weight dropped across those two and a half years of
late childhood to 80 pounds. Stanley, at 13, was 5 feet 4
inches but weighed only 97 pounds … We looked like con-
centration camp victims.[47]

How did Richard and Stanley survive? They survived because people cared. People provided a positive alternative to a negative situation. The involvement of others made all the difference. The boys not only survived, they flourished and prospered. Dr. Rhodes recalls the kindness of a grade school teacher who, despite her own modest salary, sent the boys on errands to a nearby grocery with "an extra dime" for a half-pint of milk. He remembers how a woman deep-frying doughnuts risked her job to pass them warm samples during bitterly cold winter days. An equally impoverished widow who lived in a small trailer nearby showed them kindness and understanding. Finally, when the abuse became life-threatening, Stanley found the courage to run away from home. He spent the night in the city's huge sewer tunnels, then went to the police, who rescued the boys from certain death. They were placed under the loving care and supervision of the Andrew Drumm Institute, a home for indigent boys.

Ignoring a difficult situation is never enough. Those who courageously do what is "right and just and fair" (Proverbs 1:3) achieve success. Every negative situation presents at least equal if not greater opportunity for a good solution. Christians know they are not alone. As the prophet Hanani told King Asa, "The eyes of the LORD range throughout the earth to strengthen those whose hearts are fully committed to Him" (2 Chronicles 16:9). Those who act in faith can anticipate the intervention and rescue of the Lord.

Rescue Is Possible

No situation is impossible unless it's ignored. The Lord has invited us to request His involvement. He also knows how difficult change is for people with human frailties. One of the most comforting passages of the New Testament reminds us that Jesus knows what it's like to be human. Our God in heaven once walked the earth and experienced all the trials and temptations of life. He not only witnessed the temptations of life, He *personally experienced* them. The human nature of Jesus and His life on earth is as important today as it was in the first century. The Bible says, "We do not have a high priest who is unable to sympathize with our weaknesses, but we have one who has been tempted in every way, just as we are—yet was without sin. Let us then approach the throne of grace with confidence, so that we may receive mercy and find grace to help us in our time of need" (Hebrews 4:15–16).

Those who seek the serenity that only God can give will be guided to peaceful waters and green pastures, away from destructive behaviors toward life. It is impossible to achieve lasting change by only eliminating negative behavior. Every commandment that forbids a wrong behavior also offers a godly alternative.

> "We *should fear and love God so that we do not curse, swear, use satanic arts, lie, or deceive by His name*, but call upon it in every trouble, pray, praise, and give thanks."

Or, "We should fear and love God so that we do not despise preaching and His Word, but hold it sacred and gladly hear and learn from it." Or, "We should fear and love God so that we do not despise or anger our parents and other authorities, but honor them, serve and obey them, love and cherish them." (emphasis added)[48]

God pulls us out of the mire and sets our feet on a better path. "I waited patiently for the LORD; He turned to me and heard my cry. He lifted me out of the slimy pit, out of the mud and mire; He set my feet on a rock and gave me a firm place to stand. He put a new song in my mouth, a hymn of praise to our God. Many will see and fear and put their trust in the LORD" (Psalm 40:1–3). Replacing wrong behavior with godly behavior is an important step in the right direction.

Serenity Principle 10: Eliminating Negatives Is Not Enough

Putting Principle Number 10 into Action

1. Identify the sin that troubles you most. What alternative behaviors are recommended in God's Word?
   - When tempted to commit that sin, what are three things you could do instead? (Refer to Serenity Principles 7 and 8 for additional help.)
2. Whom do you trust enough to help you with your personal struggle?
   - Ask him or her to call you or have breakfast with you once a week for the next three months.
   - During your time together, share a devotional (make sure it includes the reading of God's Word) and pray together.

- After three months you may want to maintain contact in a similar way once a month for a year.

Pray When Seeking Change

Lord, I am struggling and need Your help. I know that nothing is impossible for You. Help me to identify areas in my life that need change and give me guidance to make those changes, Lord. I read in Your Word about all the times You've given Your children a firm footing on the narrow path. Guide me and encourage me with Your favor. In Jesus' name. Amen.

Epilogue

The Essential Ingredient

No Christ, No Peace; Know Christ, Know Peace

What are the essential ingredients of a satisfied and peaceful life? Would greater financial security provide the confidence you lack? Would the assurance of good health put your mind at ease? What is the key to happiness? Is happiness a by-product of wisdom, success at work, personal recognition, common sense, emotional stability, a stable childhood, love, acceptance, and peace at home? Some would say it's a combination of all these things—no one thing results in serenity. They would be wrong.

There is one key and only one key to the serenity everyone seeks. The prophet spoke of it 600 years before the birth of Christ:

> You will keep in perfect peace him whose mind is steadfast, because he trusts in You. Trust in the LORD forever, for the LORD, the LORD, is the Rock eternal.
>
> (Isaiah 26:3–4)

Trusting in the Wrong Things

Sometimes, the most obvious answer escapes our notice. Albert Amateau has been blessed with good health and a long life. In fact, Albert Amateau is one of America's oldest citizens. But it doesn't seem like such a big deal to him. Albert says he always knew he would live beyond 100 years and consciously planned for it. One of his secrets is regular exercise. He walks three or four miles every day. When pressed by a doctor to disclose his formula for longevity, Albert mentioned his commitment to daily exercise. The physician was impressed but wanted to know more.

> *"What do you do when it rains?" asked the doctor.*
> *"I put on a raincoat," the old man replied.*[49]

Sometimes the solution to our problem is just too obvious to be believed, like the driver frantically looking for the keys she has firmly clutched in her hand, or the man searching for glasses that are resting on his nose. It happens to us all. Expecting things to be more difficult, we ignore the obvious. The search for serenity can be like that—looking for answers in all the wrong places.

Searching for serenity in all the wrong places is not a new problem. Jesus told a story about people who do just that. He had been teaching great crowds of people about the issue of trust. He said, "Are not five sparrows sold for two pennies? Yet not one of them is forgotten by God. Indeed, the very hairs of your head are all numbered. Don't be afraid; you are worth more than many sparrows" (Luke 12:6–7). Someone in the crowd thought the Lord's teaching on trust could help him benefit at the expense of his brother. The man shouted out to Jesus, "Teacher, tell my brother to divide the inheritance with me" (Luke 12:13). But instead of agreeing, Jesus challenged his attitude by reminding him and us, "Beware, and be on your guard against every form of greed; for not even when one has an abundance does his life consist of his possessions" (Luke 12:15 NASB). The importance of Jesus' remark cannot be over-emphasized: *"not even when one has an abundance* does his life consist of his possessions." Later Jesus drove the point home: "For life is more than food, and the body more than clothing" (Luke 12:23).

There Is No Serenity in the Abundance of Things

Jesus pointed out the obvious. This world is only temporary. There is no permanent result in a temporary solution. How do you measure personal success? What is the permanent solution to our temporary problems? Where does the search for serenity end?

- Is it by achieving more than your brothers or sisters?
- Is it by attending a class reunion hoping to be asked how things are going so you can brag about your great success?
- Is it by achieving more than your fraternity brothers or sorority sisters?
- Is it through the attainment of more than your parents?
- Is it in outachieving those in your office or others in your field of study?

If those are the goals in your search for serenity you need to know two things: First, when you arrive at the next level there will be people already there. Don't expect them to be especially glad to see you. Second, after you've adjusted to your new surroundings, you'll find a door leading to a staircase the ambitious climb to attain even greater success. A fellow climber once observed, "Even if you win the rat race, you're still a rat."

Jesus wanted to spare you the pain. He offered a better goal.

The Peace That Surpasses
All Understanding

What you can never achieve has been achieved for you. The outcome for Christians was assured on Calvary. After you've looked everywhere, tried everything, followed everyone, read every other book, come back to the obvious. Jesus has accomplished our peace on the cross. That was the message of the angels, "Glory to God in the highest, and on earth peace to men on whom His favor rests" (Luke 2:14). He is the Prince of Peace and the Lord of Serenity.

The search for serenity ends with Jesus. He once challenged the leaders of His day by saying, "You diligently study the Scriptures because you think that by them you possess eternal life. These are the Scriptures that testify about Me" (John 5:39). That doesn't mean Christians are shielded from hardship, nor do they escape difficulty based on the degree of their faithfulness. The value of faith is realized in struggle, and strength of joy is measured by sorrow. Jesus said, "Come to Me, all you who are weary and burdened, and I will give you rest. Take My yoke upon you and learn from Me, for I am gentle and humble in heart, and you will find rest for your souls. For My yoke is easy and My burden is light" (Matthew 11:28–30).

One of the earliest observations recorded on the value of the Christian faith was intended as an insult. The King James translation captures the essence of the accusation: "These that have turned the world upside down are come hither also" (Acts 17:6 KJV). The Greek word used to describe the impact of the Gospel literally means "to upset" or "to stir up." Jesus upset the normal way of thinking, and His followers stirred up the people they met. Their faith turned their world upside down.

A Faith You Can Bank On

You may never have heard of William Larimer Mellon Jr. He was born into the Mellon family of Pittsburgh, who achieved great wealth and fame through investment banking and the industrial revolution. But banking, manufacturing, and life on the east coast held little interest for Larry Mellon. Like the man in Jesus' story, at age 37, Larry Mellon decided to retire and take life easy. He purchased a large Arizona ranch where he intended to raise his children and supervise the breeding of fine cattle. He was about to discover the power of Jesus' words: "Life is more than food, and the body more than clothes" (Luke 12:23).

He came across an article that described how a man named Albert Schweitzer had left a successful career in music, teaching, and writing to serve as a medical missionary in Africa. Larry Mellon was fascinated by the idea of an extremely successful person giving up everything to live in virtual obscurity. He was overwhelmed by Schweitzer's decision to live the life of a servant as an act of gratitude for all that God had done for him. Mellon's own life had no meaning that remotely resembled Schweitzer's. He wrote the great doctor seeking his advice.

>Mellon wrote, "I am 37 years old; I have a family and all the responsibilities that go with it. But I want to do what you have done. What do you advise?"

>Schweitzer replied, "Many men have asked me the question you have sent, but I have been reluctant to advise them. The decision is difficult, and there are many hardships. It is the plight of the dogooders in this world that others should throw rocks in their path. But you seem courageous. I urge you to pursue your goal."[50]

Mellon felt renewed. His mission was clear. He would enroll in medical school, obtain his degree, and then offer his services in some rural part of America that could otherwise not afford a medical doctor. He could thereby combine his love of ranching with his newfound mission of service. His wife, Gwen, was skeptical, his friends thought he was experiencing an early midlife crisis, and the medical schools doubted his commitment. He was finally accepted at Tulane University and began his quest. Mellon and Schweitzer continued to exchange correspondence and twice met, once at the doctor's African hospital in Lambaréné, and later when Schweitzer returned to Europe on a lecture series. Mellon surprised everyone by his resolve.

He did his specialization on the subject of tropical ulcers. A survey of world conditions led Mellon to conduct research in Haiti, a land of immeasurable suffering and poverty. Thousands lived in the poorest of conditions. Medically treatable illnesses like tuberculosis, malaria, malnutrition, and tetanus were epidemic in Haiti. One visit was all it took to convince Dr. Mellon that Haiti, not rural America, was where the Lord was calling him to serve. On completion of his studies in 1956, Dr. Mellon used $2 million of his own money to build a modern hospital in a country where people had more confidence in voodoo, magicians, and those who talked with the dead than in modern medicine. He named his rescue mission Hospital Albert Schweitzer.

Larry and Gwen Mellon found serenity in their faith and the call of Christ into Christian service. He was a hands-on administrator with a vision for equipping others to carry on the work when he no longer could. Built and funded by foreigners, today 95 percent of Hospital Albert Schweitzer's staff are native Haitians. From the beginning, Dr. Mellon's strategy included the training and equipping of native people as an ultimate goal. Dr. Mellon died in 1989. Seven years later, Gwen

Mellon received the Haitian Medal of Honor, that nation's highest award, as recognition of their commitment to the Haitian people.[51] It wasn't really necessary; Dr. Mellon had already received his reward in full.

The Serenity Factor

Faith is God's gift to His people. If, as the prophet says, "[God keeps] in perfect peace him whose mind is steadfast because he trusts in You" (Isaiah 26:3), then it follows that as faith grows, peace also increases. But how can we increase faith if it is a gift of God? No one can make someone give them more of a gift. It would no longer qualify as a gift if it were coerced. Thankfully, God has spelled out how faith is acquired and how it grows.

The Lord gives faith to His people through the power of His Word. The Bible says, "Faith comes from hearing the message, and the message is heard through the Word of Christ" (Romans 10:17). God comes to us in His Word. God's Word has power as the Holy Spirit works through it to bring us to accept and trust God's ways. Paul described this mystery in his first letter to the Christians at Corinth.

> No one knows the thoughts of God except the Spirit of God.
> We have not received the spirit of the world but the Spirit
> who is from God, that we may understand what God has
> freely given us. This is what we speak, not in words taught
> us by human wisdom but in words taught by the Spirit,
> expressing spiritual truths in spiritual words. The man with-
> out the Spirit does not accept the things that come from the
> Spirit of God, for they are foolishness to him, and he cannot
> understand them, because they are spiritually discerned.
>
> (1 Corinthians 2:11–14)

Those who desire greater serenity should desire greater faith. Greater faith is obtained through the power of the Holy Spirit working through God's Word on the hearts of those who believe.

The Faith Connection

Faith is defined for us in the Bible as "Being sure of what we hope for and certain of what we do not see. This is what the ancients were commended for. By faith we understand that the universe was formed at God's command, so that what is seen was not made out of what was visible" (Hebrews 11:1–3).

Dr. Niebuhr's serenity prayer is a prayer of simple faith:

God, grant me the serenity to accept the things
I cannot change, courage to change the things I can,
and wisdom to know the difference.

The prayer was composed in 1934 for a sermon Dr. Niebuhr preached in a small church near his summer home in Heath, Massachusetts. After the service, a summer neighbor, Howard Chandler Robbins, asked if he could have a copy. According to Robbins, Niebuhr handed him the original saying, "Here, take the prayer. I have no further use for it."[52] But the prayer struck a nerve that would not soon be quieted. Robbins published it as part of a pamphlet the following year and it has since been adopted by various support groups and distributed to millions of servicemen in the armed forces.

Perhaps Niebuhr had no need for his sermon notes that day in 1934, but the ideas contained in the famous prayer would serve him well in the days to come. Like many Christian leaders, he was drawn into the racial equality debates of the 1950s. But what could be changed? And what should be accepted as unchangeable? Those were days when wisdom, courage, and serenity were needed in great supply.

A black woman named Rosa Parks, tired from work, refused to move to the back of a crowded bus. A stand had been taken for equality. It received national attention when a young preacher named Martin Luther King Jr. led a much publicized and controversial boycott of the city bus system. Niebuhr, a white pastor from Detroit, stood with the oppressed, calling Dr. King's courage "the most effective way of justice."[53] The storm raged, but those who stood within the will of God had peace despite the violence. It requires faith to believe that what is right is also what is best. Those who take such stands never know how things will eventually turn out, but they have the peace of knowing they are standing on solid ground. It was Franklin Roosevelt who said, "I'd rather fail at a cause that will eventually succeed, than succeed in a cause that will eventually fail."

One Day at a Time

Every day in America:

- 2,740 kids run away from home.
- 63,288 automobile accidents occur in which 129 people die.
- 5,962 couples marry, 1,986 couples divorce.
- A woman is raped every 27 minutes, and someone is robbed every 78 seconds. A thief breaks and enters every 10 seconds and a car is stolen every 33 seconds.
- People drink more than 90 million cans of beer and smoke more than 1.6 billion cigarettes.
- 2,740 teenagers become pregnant.
- 2,466 children are bitten by dogs.
- 3 bike riders are killed in accidents and 15 people drown.

- 5,100 people die, 1,070 of cancer.

- And every day in America another 9,077 babies are born, 1,282 of them to single mothers.[54]

A lot can happen in one day and it's not all good. In fact, it can be overwhelming. But, taking one day at a time is essential to our peace of mind. It was the advice Jesus gave to those who were inclined to worry. In His Sermon on the Mount, He said,

> Do not worry about your life, what you will eat or drink;
> or about your body, what you will wear. Is not life more
> important than food, and the body more important than
> clothes? Look at the birds of the air; they do not sow or
> reap or store away in barns, and yet your heavenly
> Father feeds them. Are you not much more valuable
> than they? Who of you by worrying can add a single
> hour to his life? And why do you worry about clothes?
> See how the lilies of the field grow. They do not labor
> or spin. Yet I tell you that not even Solomon in all his
> splendor was dressed like one of these. If that is how
> God clothes the grass of the field, which is here today and
> tomorrow is thrown into the fire, will He not much more
> clothe you, O you of little faith? So do not worry, saying,
> "What shall we eat?" or "What shall we drink?" or
> "What shall we wear?" For the pagans run after all these
> things, and your heavenly Father knows that you need
> them. But seek first His kingdom and his righteousness,
> and all these things will be given to you as well. Therefore
> do not worry about tomorrow, for tomorrow will worry
> about itself. Each day has enough trouble of its own.
>
> (Matthew 6:25–34)

Again the Lord reminds us of the obvious. But just like Mr. Amateau and his raincoat, sometimes it's important to restate the obvious. Jesus' formula for dealing with worry was simple and direct:

1. Worry never changed anything.
2. God takes excellent care of less important things than you—and He does it every day.
3. Unbelievers worry because they don't know God. His children should have a different perspective.
4. Our task today is to please the Father, doing what He wants done, enjoying the gift of His perfect righteousness.
5. Live in the present.

The past is behind you. You can't go back even if you wanted to. You can't go forward to escape the present. You can only live in the present. The future is guaranteed to no one. You must take each day as it comes. *Today* you can agree that worry is a waste of time. *Today* you can correct the mistakes of your past. *Today* you can make your apologies and change your direction. *Today* you can forgive the wrongs and move on, but you can't undo what has been done. *Today* you can begin again. *Today* you can see a sparrow and remember how much God loves you. *Today* you can seek God's direction. *Today* you can live in the knowledge of His love and forgiveness. *Today* you can make your plans, remembering to add, "If it is God's will." *Today* is yours to learn from your yesterdays and plan for your tomorrows. *Today* is the most important day of your life.

Taking Stock and Taking Action

How will you spend your day? Let the *Serenity Principles* give you direction. Every day acknowledge these truths:

1. Everything changes except God.
2. You can expect opposition.
3. You can know what is best, right, and true.
4. Honesty must precede change.
5. God can change people.
6. God can change situations.
7. God's Word is a change agent.
8. There is power in prayer.
9. It is not good for man to be alone.
10. Eliminating negatives is not enough.

Jesus said, "I have come that they may have life, and have it to the full" (John 10:10). If your life lacks serenity, it is not the life the Lord intends for you. He offers peace you will find nowhere else. The night He was arrested and tried, He told His disciples, "Peace I leave with you; My peace I give you. I do not give to you as the world gives. Do not let your hearts be troubled and do not be afraid" (John 14:27). He is the Good Shepherd. He knows you by name and will lead you to the peaceful waters and green pastures. He is "the way and the truth and the life" (John 14:6). The key to serenity is not the end of trouble, it is the beginning of faith.

> *I have told you these things, so that in Me you may have peace. In this world you will have trouble. But take heart! I have overcome the world.*   (John 16:33)

The Serenity Principles: Putting Faith into Action

1. The Christian is ruled in his or her actions by either flesh or spirit (see Romans 7:18 and Romans 8:1–17).

Theologians describe it as being "sinner" and "saint" at the same time. Paul said if you sow to the spirit you will harvest eternal life, but if you sow to the flesh you will harvest destruction. What temptations are making demands on your life? How do you handle them?

2. How do you live each day?
   - What pattern do you follow?
   - How do you make sure you control your day and not the other way around?
   - How is your faith in Christ reflected in your day's schedule?

Pray for the Proper Perspective

Lord, You are the one thing needful. I must admit that if You visited me like the day you visited Martha and Mary, you might find me "worried and troubled about many things." I want to be more like Mary. I want to choose the one thing needful. Help me overcome my sinful tendencies. Thank You for Your Word. Thank You for sending the Holy Spirit to give power to Your people. As I commit myself to Your leading and as I study Your Word give me the peace I seek, the peace that can be found nowhere else. Empower my witness and give wisdom to my words so that others might be drawn to You. I commend myself to You, the Author and Finisher of my faith. Amen.

Endnotes

1 "No Growth," *The American Spectator*, January 1984.

2 W.G. Polack, *The Handbook to the Lutheran Hymnal*, (St. Louis, Missouri: Concordia Publishing House, 1942) 539.

3 Text: Henry F. Lyte, 1793–1847, "Abide with Me," hymn 490:3, *Lutheran Worship*, © Copyright 1982 by Concordia Publishing House, St. Louis, Missouri. All rights reserved.

4 Ibid., 490:5.

5 Polack, page 540.

6 Michael Jackson, "Man in the Mirror," Glen Ballard, MCA Music Publishing and Seidah Garrett, Yellowbrick Road Music, c/o Warner Chappell Records. Used by permission.

7 Charles R. Swindoll, Growing Strong in the Seasons of Life, (Portland, Oregon: Multnomah Press, 1983).

8 Elisabeth Kübler Ross, *On Death and Dying*,(New York, New York: Collier Books, Macmillan Publishing Company, 1969).

9 Ralph Killmann and Tersa Covin, "The Change Process," *The Pryor Report*, Volume 7, 1a.

10 Lowell Lundstrom, "My Precious Prodigal: What I Learned from My Daughter's 9-year Plunge into Prostitution," *New Man Magazine*, November/December, 1996, page 63. Used by permission.

11 Ibid., 64.

12 Ibid., 66.

13 Text: Martin Luther, 1483–1546; tr. composite. "A Mighty Fortress Is Our God," hymn 298:2, *Lutheran Worship*, © Copyright 1982 by Concordia Publishing House, St. Louis, Missouri. All rights reserved.

14 For more information on Burma Shave, see *Reminisce Magazine*, July/August 1994, pages 60–61.

15 Merle Miller, *Plain Speaking: An Oral Biography of Harry S. Truman*, (New York, New York: Berkley Publishing Corporation, 1973, 1974) 142.

16 Samuel Gallu, *Give 'Em Hell Harry*, (New York, New York: Avon Books, 1975) 110.

17 Miller, 251.

18 Carl S. Meyer, Editor, *Walther Speaks to the Church: Selected Letters by C. F. W. Walther*, (St. Louis, Missouri: Concordia Publishing House, 1973) 38.

19 David was first anointed by Samuel in 1 Samuel 16:13. After Saul's death on Mount Gilboa (1 Samuel 31), David was anointed King of the south in Hebron (2 Samuel 2). Abner, commander of Saul's armies placed Ish-Bosheth (Saul's son) on the throne of his father in the North for seven years. Only after Ish-Bosheth's assassination by commanders of his own army was David finally anointed king over all of Israel (2 Samuel 5).

20 Polack, 193.

21 Mimi Brodsky Chenfeld, "Words of Praise: Honey on the Page," *Language Arts*, volume 62, number 3, March 1985. Copyright 1998 by the National Council of Teachers of English. Reprinted with permission.

22 Vernon E. Johnson, *I'll Quit Tomorrow*, (New York, New York: Harper & Row Publishers, Inc. 1973) 49–51.

23 Elaine Viets, "They're Gifted at Being Average," St. Louis, Missouri: *St. Louis Post Dispatch*, November 17, 1987. Reprinted with permission of the St. Louis Post-Dispatch, copyright 1987.

24 H. Norman Schwarzkopf, from a speech made in St. Louis, Missouri during the Success 1994 Conference, November 10, 1994.

25 Corrie ten Boom with John and Elizabeth Sherrill, *The Hiding Place*, (Chappaqua, New York: Chosen Books, 1971) page viii. Used by permission.

26 Ibid., 198–199.

27 Ibid., 238.

28 Ibid., 138.

29 Corrie ten Boom with C. C. Carlson, *In My Father's House*, (Old Tappan, New Jersey: Fleming H. Revell Company, 1976) 85.

30 Not everyone would agree with Mark's assessment of MacArthur's Korea legacy. No doubt he inflamed opposition by pressing for permission to wage a more extensive war against the communists' support of North Korean aggression. He was relieved of his command by president Truman for being (in Truman's words) "Unable to give his wholehearted support to the policies of the United States Government and the United Nations."

31 General Courtney Whitney, *MacArthur: His Rendezvous with History*, (New York, New York: Knopf, 1955).

32 Booker T. Washington, *Up from Slavery*, (New York, New York: Penguin Books, 1986) 39–40.

33 Methuselah is estimated to be the oldest of all living trees. It is a bristlecone pine estimated to be 4,600 years old and growing in the California White Mountains.

34 Paul Lee Tan, *Encyclopedia of 7,700 Illustrations: Signs of the Times*, (Chicago, Illinois: Donnelley and Sons, Inc., 1979) 1499.

35 Text: Martin Luther, 1483–1546; tr. composite. "A Mighty Fortress Is Our God," hymn 298:3, *Lutheran Worship*, © Copyright 1982 by Concordia Publishing House, St. Louis, Missouri. All rights reserved.

36 Charles Dickens, *The Christmas Books of Charles Dickens*, (Ann Arbor, Michigan: Tally Hall Press, 1996) page 68.

37 Ibid.

38 *Luther's Small Catechism with Explanation*, (St. Louis, Missouri: Concordia Publishing House, 1986) 18.

39 Attributed to Reinhold Niebuhr.

40 Norman Vincent Peale, *A Guide to Confident Living*, (New York, New York: Prentice-Hall Inc., 1948) 96.

41 Peggy Anderson, compiler, *Great Quotes from Great Leaders*, (Lombard, Illinois: Celebrating Excellence Publishing, 1990) 55.

42 Pat McMillen of Team Resource Incorporated speaking at a Leadership Training conference at Willow Creek Community Church, South Barrington, Illinois, 1997.

43 John Maxwell, *Developing the Leaders around You*, (Nashville, Tennessee: Thomas Nelson Publishers, 1995) 11.

44 Used by permission of Sister Helen P. Mrosla.

45 Tom Neven, "General Principles," *Focus on the Family Magazine*, November 1997.

46 Ibid.

47 Dr. Richard Rhodes, "Don't Be a Bystander" Parade Magazine, October 14, 1990. Reprinted with permission from Parade, copyright ©1990.

48 From Martin Luther's explanations of the second, third, and fourth Commandments. *Luther's Small Catechism with Explanation*, (St. Louis, Missouri: Concordia Publishing House, 1986) 9–10.

49 Salli Rasberry and Padi Selwyn, *Living Your Life Out Loud*, (New York, New York: Pocket Books, 1995) 109.

50 Glenn D. Kittler, "The Man Who Forgot Himself," *The Guideposts Treasury of Faith*, (Carmel, New York: Guideposts Magazine, 1970) 420–421.

51 "Equity and Access: Haitian Hospital Reaches Out to Families and Communities," *The W.K. Kellogg Foundation International Journal*, volume 7, number 2.

52 June Bingham, *Courage to Change: An Introduction to the Life and Thought of Reinhold Niebuhr*, (New York, New York: Charles Scribner's Sons, 1972).

53 Ibid., 110.

54 Mike Finsilber and William B. Mead, *American Averages: Amazing Facts of Everyday Life*, (New York, New York: Doubleday Publishers, 1980).